Brothers

Ireland & Israel

MIKE HARPER

ISBN-13: **978-1-9163722-8-3**

If you would like to contact the author, please email us at

mike@revivalwell.org

www.RevivalWell.org

A window of light,
Where once my brother was lined up,
Came forth a new window of hope.
Here he was once persecuted,
But here too was he founded.
Oh Israel, thou are born again

Basel, 15 Mar 2017

CONTENTS

Dedicated to my wife, Edith

FOREWORD

Basel

I had upon occasion, come across references to Jews in Irish and Celtic history. Whenever I did, I prayed and asked the Lord that He would revisit the topic with me. In 2017, that journey or 'turas' began. I remember it clearly. It happened during an intercession mission. I had taken several trips to countries across Europe. But on this trip, I had flown into Basel heading for Strasbourg to pray at the EU buildings there. On the return journey, I had to stop for an overnight in Basel before the flight in the morning.

I had never been to Basel before or indeed to Switzerland at all. I got off the train and walked down towards the centre of the city. I had drawn a rough map on a piece of paper to help guide me to the hotel. But I could not locate it, forcing me to switch on the roaming on my phone to direct me. I had to back-track a little, go down another street and there it was. I checked in and settled into the room. I had researched the history of Basel briefly before my trip and had read about the persecution of Jews there and so on, but as I stepped up to look out my hotel window, right across the street I noticed something, it was the Stadtcasino.

Why on earth would a concert hall, of all things, be of interest to a travelling intercessor. The building wasn't thrilling itself, but more the history of what happened there. It was the place where the very first Zionist Congress took place in 1897. Perhaps the reestablishment of the nation of Israel had begun here. At the very least, it was an event which brought international attention to Zionism. It was not long before I found myself downstairs and then across the street to get a closer look. At the time, it was undergoing renovation and had notices up saying ‘closed’. There was one section of the building open and occupied by a tourist office. I went inside to enquire. The receptionist confirmed that due to the renovations I would not be able to go inside. I was a little sad but curious as to why the Lord had led me here to this particular place.

With that in mind, I went for a walk around the area. Adjacent to the concert hall is a large church, but I did not enter it. I walked downhill towards the river, to walk across the 'Middle Bridge', and just to pray and seek the Lord. Both thanking Him for a successful mission to Strasbourg but also asking Him if there was something in Basel for me. I remember that when I returned to the hotel, I stayed up late, looking out that window and praying.

Early in the morning, I packed my things and left the hotel. I felt drawn to go back to the Stadcasino, this time I went down the side of it and surprisingly found an old door, a side entrance. It was directly opposite to a side door of the church. Led by the Lord, I took out my faithful tin whistle and began to worship the Lord. The beautiful sound echoed away through the quiet Sunday morning streets. Some pedestrians stopped to listen to the music. I stood directly between the two doors and worshipped God. I knew what this meant. The door on my right represented the Jews, Zionism and the foundation of Israel. The other entrance to my left was symbolic of the church. These two doors were closed. They had no interest in hearing each other. It was closed, but yet, I felt a desire to be a witness to their reconciliation.

Dublin

The following spring, there was a gathering of believers arranged at the National Boxing Arena in Dublin. The focus of the meeting was to pray for Ireland regarding the upcoming vote on abortion. While the day of prayer has little to do with Israel, something happened at the end of the meeting. An Israeli man was invited into the stage to let out a few blasts from his shofar. It may have just been for a few moments but, I had a strange vision. I saw two brothers standing on the beach, they both had a flag wrapped around them, or maybe they were wearing a jersey with the flag colours. In the distance and to their right was a sea point. They stood side by side with an arm around each other's shoulders, and I saw a caption 'brothers'. It was then that I knew that I would write a book, but I did not start to research yet, I just waited on the Lord. Twice before, the Lord has called me on journeys about Irish history, to research then visit specific places and to pray. I want to express that I have no natural interest in history. Both of those times, the Holy Spirit stirred up a deep hunger in my heart to research, and as I did, knowledge and revelation came. As these events began to surface, I knew that I would need to wait for the Lord to do the same once again, and He did.

In January 2019, my wife and I travelled up to Dublin for a weekend of ministry. On Saturday, we went out to Malahide to meet up with an intercessor called Katey. She was beginning a new prayer journey across Ireland, which involved a marathon, worship and prayer in every county of Ireland. We had heard about the events and were considering helping when they would be coming through Laois in March. We felt it on our hearts though, to support the first one by helping with the worship at the end of the marathon. We met the marathon runners at the finish line. Then we went for a walk to the base of the town to pray. Afterwards, we gathered down at the beach to worship God. We were about to finish when another couple turned up to join in. They had brought national flags of Ireland and Israel. I did not notice the flags at first, but when I did, I suddenly remembered the vision I had a year previous of two brothers with the flags standing on a beach. I asked them about the flags, and they shared that the Holy Spirit had been specific in asking them to bring the flags along. Then I told them about my vision, and we proceeded to take a photo or two. For me, this signalled an activation to go.

> "I have in former years often declared that the Three Evil Influences of the century were the Pirate, the Freemason, and the Jew"
>
> Arthur Griffiths, founder of Sinn Féin

AN IRISH ROLE IN ZIONISM
CHAPTER 1

I think it best to start with a definition of Zionism itself. Its meaning is hotly debated in our modern political arena, and many people attempt to redefine it to suit their own beliefs. The traditional view is expressed by the Oxford Dictionary which defines Zionism as a "movement for (originally) the re-establishment and (now) the development and protection of a Jewish nation in what is now Israel. It was established as a political organization in 1897 under Theodor Herzl, and was later led by Chaim Weizmann"[1]. On the other side of the debate, there are supporters of 'Palestine' who wish to redefine and rewrite history. For example, the Urban Dictionary now defines a Zionist as "A race supremacist, colonialist, extremist. One who believes in a political ideology that hijacked Judaism, soon to hijack Christianity[2]."

The question underlying the Zionism debate, is, do Jews have the right to the land of Israel? Your answer will most likely influence your definition and political stance towards Israel. In this chapter, I hope to express some of the historical roles that Ireland has played in the re-establishment, development and protection of Israel. I believe that the history involved is vital to modern Ireland and very much ignored by our society and politicians. It is only fair to state from the outset that I support

---

1 The Oxford Dictionary of Phrase and Fable (2 ed.), Oxford University Press, 9780198609810.

2 'Zionist' [Online] Urban Dictionary, https://www.urbandictionary.com/define.php?term=zionist

Israel and their right to exist. I wouldn't stand over everything that the nation does. Still, my support for their right to exist goes deeply into my heart and mind. Especially so, given the historical similarities that both Ireland and Israel share.

Firstly, we should consider that the concept of a 'people' or a 'nation' originates from God. Apostle Luke wrote, *"he made from one man every nation of mankind to live on all the face of the earth, having determined allotted periods and the boundaries of their dwelling place"* Acts 17:26 ESV. The Old Testament follows the history of the covenant promise to Abraham that his descendants will inherit the 'promised land'. But there are plenty of examples of God's hand upon other nations. We see the influence of God impacting Egypt and Pharaoh during Joseph's time and at the time of the Exodus. God's power over Babylon must be noted too during the time of Daniel as one ruler is removed, and another installed during a single night. We see the 'promised land' also given over to the Israelites as a judgement upon the people who lived there.

We cannot ignore this point. God has appointed nations and their boundaries. He is deeply involved in their history, just as much as the history of Israel. Yes, it was through Abraham that covenant came, and yes, it was to these people and their land that Jesus would come. But Jesus sacrifice was not aimed at just one people or nation, but to the whole world. God chose Israel to be His instrument to reach other countries. The nations were always supposed to be involved in the story, and to some extent, they were. We will be discussing the role the Gentiles played in later Chapters.

Secondly, we must ponder if mankind can change the plans and purposes of God for the nations. And if God establishes rulers and nations, then what is our role - are we just to sit back and be spectators to history? My initial thought is that yes, people do interfere with God's purposes. After the intercessory mission in 2017, I realized that the EU project is mostly the work of witchcraft and a re-establishment of the Babylon ideals. If God established Ireland's existence as a nation, then the work of the EU is undoubtedly eroding the nations existence, borders and purpose. However, I should consider that I am viewing these events from within history.

God is not subject to time and space and can view the beginning and end of our history, so He has made provision for both good and bad.

The apostle Paul said that *"we know that for those who love God all things work together for good, for those who are called according to his purpose"* Rom 8:28 ESV. Knowing that God has already seen the future should give us hope, but not complacency. We are not outside of time but are actively involved with what is happening. I like a phrase from a well-known movie which says that we are not here to make decisions, but here to understand the choices that we have already made. What good would it have done if Paul had declared 'God is in control' and had not gone out on his apostolic journeys to reach the world? God's foreknowledge does not make us exempt but instead makes us part of the story. Paul went on to say, *"For those whom he foreknew he also predestined to be conformed to the image of his Son, in order that he might be the firstborn among many brothers. And those whom he predestined he also called, and those whom he called he also justified, and those whom he justified he also glorified"* Rom 8:9-10 ESV.

So, what then is our role in the situation where our nations and rulers fall into corruption? I believe that when corruption manifests, whether it be in a country or a religious organization, it occurs as a judgement upon the people for what is in their hearts. The answer is not rebellion[3]. The answer is repentance, prayer, faith, hope and reconciliation. Surely, we should have a similar stance to the nations that we do to non-believers – hoping that they will repent and embrace the Lord, love Him and obey Him. I believe that our job is one of reconciliation, acting in obedience to the Lord and looking for opportunities to intercede and witness the restoration of people and nations.

So, what then is the God-ordained purpose for the Jews? They had such a wonderful covenant promise, but when Jesus came to fulfil what had been foretold by the prophets, He was rejected. Was their purpose then lost? Apostle Paul pondered these things deeply, being a Jew who had denied Jesus initially but then accepted Him wholeheartedly. He states clearly in his writings that God has not rejected the Jews[4]. Instead, Paul points out that God always saves for himself a remnant despite many Jews hardening their hearts[5]. He also foresees a day, after the fullness of the Gentiles has been brought in, when the Jews

---

3 See Romans 3:1-5.

4 See Romans 11:1-2.

5 Jesus wept for Jerusalem at their rejection, and prophesied as to their future trouble, see Luke 19:41-44.

may yet in large numbers accept Jesus. He puts it like this, *"And even they, if they do not continue in their unbelief, will be grafted in, for God has the power to graft them in again"* Rom 11:23 ESV. The hope then for the unbelieving Jews is that they are grafted back in.

I believe that the day of grafting back in began with the restoration of Israel. As believers, we believe that Jesus will return. But Jesus' return is dependent upon the Jews possessing Israel. When lamenting for the city, He spoke over Jerusalem saying, *"For I tell you that you will not see Me again until you say, 'Blessed is He who comes in the name of the Lord'"* Matt 28:39 ESV. To strongly support my point are the growing numbers of Messianic believers in Israel since 1948, something which has been studied by the Israel College of the Bible[6]. In the chart below, you will see that the *"growth has not been linear, but exponential. Similarly, attitudes towards Messianic believers have also come a long way. Israeli Jews used to be mortified at the thought of a Jew who believed in Yeshua, but today almost everyone we talk to have heard of this growing movement of people."*[7]

Year	Population	Qty Messianic believers (estimated)	Qty Congregations	Percentage congregation leaders who are native to Israel (estimate)
1948	600,000	23	0	0%
1989	3,500,000	1,200	30	0%
1999	4,800,000	5,000	81	20%
2017	-	30,000	300	~90%

Unfortunately, many people in societies across the world degrade the importance of Israel and the Jews. Within Christian circles,

---

6 'Findings Of New Research On The Messianic Movement In Israel' [Online] OneForIsrael https://www.oneforisrael.org/bible-based-teaching-from-israel/findings-of-new-research-on-the-messianic-movement-in-israel/

7 Ibid.

there is a teaching of the so-called 'replacement theology'. They sift through the Bible, take every promise that God made to Israel, and insert their own names. It is something which is sadly not on the discernment radar of most churchgoers. But this is not a new thing, its roots go back through history as far as the Crusades and perhaps further to the Council of Nicaea. It teaches that the Jews rejected and killed Jesus and so they, in turn, should be blamed.

Irish Zionism

At the turn of the 19th century, Europe changed dramatically. Napoleon had hoped to defeat the Ottoman rulers and cut off its link to Britain and its empire. He invited Jews, as a representative of France, to reclaim their nation as "rightful heirs of Palestine"[8]. Around this time, a Hebrew Christian called Joseph Frey arrived to serve the London Missionary Society, but his heart was moved by the plight of the Jews in the city. In 1809 he founded the London Jews Society (LJS) whose primary aim was to reach Jews with the gospel message. If Zionism was a snowball gathering momentum as it rolls down a hill, this is the point where it began to move. In 1824, Edward Irving was invited by the London Missionary Society to preach. His teaching was a premillennial viewpoint, and he held prophetic views about Israel.

There was a great interest in his teachings, and so annual conferences were held at Albury House until 1830. Most attendees were Anglican, Moravian, and Church of Scotland ministers. Another attendee was Lady Powerscourt, who would travel from Ireland to England to hear well-known preachers[9]. Studies of prophecies surrounding Israel formed an essential part of the conferences. This connection is probably what let her to host 'The Prophetic conferences' at Powerscourt from 1830-1833 during difficult times in Ireland[10]. They were led by J. N. Darby and

---

8 Sixer, S. (2012) 'The Road to Balfour: The History of Christian Zionism', The Balfour Project, 24 Nov 2012.

9 Brown, J H. (2008) 'Whose faith follow: Lady Powerscourt (1800-1836)', Believer's Magazine [Online] http://www.believersmagazine.com/bm.php?i=20081211

10 The summer of 1830 brought with it a potato crop failure, and food prices began to rise. In Munster, people began to starve, and typhus fever began to spread quickly. In desperation, people went to extremes to try and feed their families. Riots broke out in places such as Limerick, mostly involving people raiding food stores and production

ministers and laypersons were invited from all over Ireland. While they were not long-lasting, Darby went on to have an influence in several European countries and the United States. He became a leading figure of Christian Zionism – a voice which began to be heard in Ireland.

Another significant influence on Zionism was an Irish man called Michael Davitt. He was a child of Irish troubles. Born in 1846, he was only four when his family was evicted from their home. He emigrated with his family as far as the UK where he later lost his arm at a cotton mill at age eleven. After recovering, a local philanthropist paid for his education[11]. But his life turned towards the Irish republican movement, a step which resulted in his imprisonment for several years. After this failure and during a time of the 1879 famine, he became a founder of the Irish National Land League to help drive reform in land rights for workers. He also drifted into politics and was twice elected to Parliament (in London). From there, his speeches made an untold amount of difference to the world, both inspiring a young Gandhi and later Martin Luther King Jr with his ideals.

In 1903, Davitt travelled to Kishinev in the Russian Empire and became one of the first journalists to witness and report on the Kishinev pogrom. He later published a book called *Within the Pale: The true Story of Anti-Semitic Persecutions in Russia*. In the book, he states his support for Zionism – that the answer to the 'Jewish Question' was the same as the answer to the 'Irish Question' – national independence. I believe that Davitt was a man who had empathy for those who were being oppressed, a man with a passion for social justice. But he did not always side with Jews and did believe some cultural stereotypes about them. However, his influence on Zionism was substantial. Davitt became like a folk hero among the Jews and had plays written about him in English and Yiddish[12].

From these two examples, we are beginning to see that Irish people contributed to the re-establishment of Israel as a State. This influence was both in spiritual and political aspects. It is perhaps worth noting that one political opponent of Davitt was Balfour as he became

---

facilities.

11 At a Methodist school.

12 Zipperstein, Steven J. (2015). "Inside Kishinev's Pogrom: Hayyim Nahman Bialik, Michael Davitt, and the Burdens of Truth" (PDF). In Freeze, ChaeRan Y.; Fried, Sylvia Fuks; Sheppard, Eugene R. (eds.). The Individual in History: Essays in Honor of Jehuda Reinharz. Waltham, Massachusetts: Brandeis University Press. ISBN 9781611687330. PP372.

Chief Secretary for Ireland in 1887. Both were keen debaters and often went head-to-head. Interestingly, Balfour was raised in an evangelical home which was sympathetic to Zionism[13], but part of me wonders if he was also influenced in part by the words of Davitt. Others undoubtedly influenced Balfour including Chaim Weizmann[14] and Lord Shaftesbury[15].

In the words of Davitt, *"It is some eighteen years since I rode from Mount Carmel to Nazareth, thence to Tiberias, and back through the beautiful plain of Jezreel, down to Nablus in Samaria on the way to Jerusalem. Jericho, the wilds of Judea, the country to the west, across the pastoral lands of Sharon, were also visited. I found the German templar colonies at Haifa, Nablus, and Sarona wearing all the appearance of comfortable clusters of garden and farming homesteads. The Jews of Bessarabia are as sober and, at least, as intelligent as these German emigrants. They have progressed in South Russia when permitted to cultivate the land. Why should they not be able to grow grain in Galilee, fruit and olives in Samaria, meat in the mountains of Judea, and wine and other products congenial to the soil and climate in the vale of Sharon, and elsewhere, in a land which flowed rich with milk and honey?*[16]*"*

An Irish role in Developing Israel

In 1918, just a year after the Balfour declaration, a baby boy was born to a Jewish family in Cliftonpark Avenue in Belfast. His name was Chaim Herzog. His father Yitzhak was soon to become Chief Rabbi of Ireland[17] and would later become the Chief Rabbi of Palestine. He could speak fluent Irish despite being born in Poland, and he was known as "the Sinn Féin Rabbi"[18] because of his support for the Irish Republican cause. After his appointment as Chief Rabbi in Ireland, the family moved to

---

13 He believed in dispensationalism which traces back to John Nelson Darby and his teachings.

14 A Jew born in the Russian Empire who became Israel's first president.

15 "Lord Shaftesbury (1801-1885) became convinced that the restoration of the Jews to Palestine was not only predicted in the Bible, but also coincided with the strategic interests of British foreign policy." See: Sixer, S. (2012) 'The Road to Balfour: The History of Christian Zionism', The Balfour Project, 24 Nov 2012.

16 Davitt, M. (1903) Within the Pale: The true Story of Anti-Semitic Persecutions in Russia.

17 1919 to 1937.

18 Benson, Asher (2007). Jewish Dublin. Dublin: A&A Farmer Ltd. p. 22. ISBN 978-1-906353-00-1.

Dublin and Chaim studied at Wesley college, but his first *"vivid memory in Dublin was of the Irish civil war"*[19] . His family then uprooted to Palestine in the 1930s, there Chaim joined the Hagenah as a guard. Their job was to secretly patrol the streets to protect Jewish communities from Arab attacks. If any were caught by the British, it *"meant a long prison term or even a death sentence"*[20]. Out of concern, his parents convinced Chaim to enrol at the University of London. After his studies and at the outbreak of war, he joined the British army[21].

He was soon transferred to complete Intelligence Corps Training and then to the officers' training school, graduating as an intelligence officer[22]. His first posting was Northern Ireland, then Sussex, and later became part of the POW interrogation unit. But he did go to Europe, and he was part of the first allied formation to cross into Germany. As news of concentration camps broke in international media, Chaim saw it with his own eyes, his first encounter of this evil happened at a *"small concentration camp just outside Bremen"*[23].

After the war ended, he continued to serve with the army until 1947. After this, he returned to Palestine, which was on the brink of war itself. Chaim wrote later about how his great-grandmother barely escaped attacks from Arabs and that their *"feelings were all too clearly expressed in periodic and horrendous mass riots in 1920, 1929*[24]*, and 1936.*[25]*"* The British had agreed to withdraw from the nation and allow Israel to become a State. I don't think they ever expected the Jews to achieve it though, as the Arabs vastly outnumbered them. Chaim wrote about his experiences through this troubled time, watching friends die to his left and right, and being injured himself.

At a vital point in these events, he struggled with the

---

19 Herzog, C. (1996) Living history, Phoenix, a division of Orion Books Ltd, London, ISBN: 075380199X, pp11.

20 Ibid, pp25.

21 He joined on 17th Dec 1942 - Herzog, C. (1996) Living history, Phoenix, a division of Orion Books Ltd, London, ISBN: 075380199X, pp46.

22 Herzog, C. (1996) Living history, Phoenix, a division of Orion Books Ltd, London, ISBN: 075380199X, pp47-49.

23 Ibid, pp61.

24 "during the Arab massacre of August 1929, in which part of Hebron's Jewish population was destroyed, many of its students were killed" - Herzog, C. (1996) Living history, Phoenix, a division of Orion Books Ltd, London, ISBN: 075380199X, pp27.

25 Herzog, C. (1996) Living history, Phoenix, a division of Orion Books Ltd, London, ISBN: 075380199X, pp23.

incompetence of the intelligence provided to the fighters. In his heart, he had a resolve and a desire to see factual and useful data helping soldiers on the front line. This resolve would soon open up to him being "one of the principal architects of the brand-new Israeli military intelligence organization"[26] . Here his experience with the British army was a key factor. He became the head of Israeli intelligence not once, but twice. After this, he eventually went into politics and eventually became the President of Israeli, serving two five-year terms.

After researching his life, I believe that Chaim was not only an interesting man but one protected [27] [28] [29] and destined by God as an Irishman to help the Israeli cause. A bold statement, but what shocks me is that so few people in my generation have even heard of him. There were, of course, others who cast their influence. Another example would be Solomon Goldberg, born in Limerick and later became *a "significant figure in the Zionist movement"*[30] .

A Future Role for Ireland

It was clear to me that the Lord was opening my heart to hear what He had to say on Ireland's role towards Jews. It was a journey which would take me across Ireland, to Europe, and eventually to Israel. The wonderful thing was that the Lord connected me with others who also during the same season were also being led on mission regarding the very same purpose. Which was of course reconciliation between Ireland and

---

26 Herzog, C. (1996) Living history, Phoenix, a division of Orion Books Ltd, London, ISBN: 075380199X, pp101.

27 In early 1947, he lost his seat on a plane to someone else who had a higher priority. Chaim shared that being "bumped from that flight not only threw me into the arms of my future wife but saved my life. The plane crashed in Tobruk." - Herzog, C. (1996) Living history, Phoenix, a division of Orion Books Ltd, London, ISBN: 075380199X, pp74.

28 His wife had a narrow escape in 1948 and had to be rushed to an ambulance, Chaim writing later said "to this day, she has many scars in her scalp" Herzog, C. (1996) Living history, Phoenix, a division of Orion Books Ltd, London, ISBN: 075380199X, pp86.

29 Chaim was also wounded, inside the French consulate during 1948. He records afterwards that "When I saw Aura that night, I realized that when I left her to go to the French consulate that morning, she had not expected to see me alive again." Herzog, C. (1996) Living history, Phoenix, a division of Orion Books Ltd, London, ISBN: 075380199X, pp93.

30 Keogh, D. (1998) 'Jews in Twentieth-Century Ireland', Cork University Press, pp13.

Israel so that the way is made for Ireland to one day stand in the gap for Jewish refugees. These unconnected teams came to Ireland in Autumn 2019.

Later, when I travelled to Israel, I met several Irish teams who had also travelled at the same time as me to Israel – again with a similar purpose in mind. The Lord was doing something much bigger than my own journey. He was arranging for that purpose to be fulfilled. Right now, God is putting these things in place. Some people are preparing their houses with more beds than they need, and they don't even know why yet. But it is because, one day, they will be a safe house for the Jews as they travel through. What a fantastic opportunity for us to redeem the behaviour of the past. It is my hope and prayer that we will do just that.

So, I believe that Ireland will have a chance for redemption, a time where we will have the opportunity to reach out and assist the Jewish community as they flee persecution. They will likely land on the West coast. Irish people will open their homes to them as they travel through this nation.

THE IRISH BOYCOTT
CHAPTER 2

Ballinrobe, Mayo

It was February, and I could feel the excitement and challenge of the new journey. At work, out of the blue, my manager asked me to go up to Westport to help with a stocktake and I reluctantly agreed. When I got there, I was also gloomy about the lack of professionalism in its organisation. I was reacting in the flesh. I was distracted. I was frustrated. I was up there for two days with an overnight stay. A couple of days later, I was asked yet again by my boss to return to Mayo. Once again, I was feeling put out but agreed to go. It was that evening when I happened across the information about Ballinrobe and boycotts. Ballinrobe was one of the towns that I had to pass through on the route to Mayo. So, I suddenly realised that it was not my worldly boss that was sending me to the area, but it was God so that He could draw my attention to Ballinrobe. I ate some humble pie.

Charles Cunningham Boycott was born on 12th March 1832[31]. He served in the British Army, which brought him to Ireland. Upon retirement from the army, he took up a position as a land agent for Lord Erne John Crichton, a landowner in Mayo. It was here that his name would become world-famous. Irish society was changing quickly. The

---

31 Wikipedia (2019) 'Charles Boycott' [online] https://en.m.wikipedia.org/wiki/Charles_Boycott (accessed 22nd Feb 2019).

Great Famine had utterly decimated the Irish population. For those who remained and survived, they were aware of how unfair the English ruled our society. A considerable part of this was the land issue. Irish farmers had been unable to buy land which had resulted in poverty. There was little choice but to be subservient to landowners, many of whom had kicked out hundreds of families from their homes during the famine.

As for Charles Boycott, he became a victim of the Land League. Boycott had arranged for a process server to be accompanied by the police to serve evictions. But a mob attacked them forcing them to take shelter in a nearby residence. After this, the local community of Ballinrobe refused to deal with Boycott at all. All the servants at his house quit, and all the local farmers refused to help him. He called in assistance with men coming from the North to gather in the harvest. It cost over ten thousand pounds to reap a crop worth five hundred pounds. Within twenty years, the word 'boycott' entered the English dictionary.

The very first public sitting of a court session under the authority of the Dáil took place in Ballinrobe on 17th May 1920[32]. In a Dáil debate the following August, the event had been described as "the cornerstone of our Judiciary"[33]. The landowners refused to adhere to the authority of the Dáil after the court judgement. That was until "the captain of the local company of the I.R.A. descended upon them with a squad of his men—sons of very poor farmers like themselves—arrested four of them and brought them off to that very effective Republican prison—an 'unknown destination.' This killed the resistance, and the prisoners were very glad to get back to their homes somewhat later, chastened and wiser men"[34]. Is this then the cornerstone of our Judiciary – that of a land of dispute and violence?

32 Oireachtas (1921) 'Dáil Éireann debate - Wednesday, 17 Aug 1921' [Online] https://www.oireachtas.ie/en/debates/debate/dail/1921-08-17/16/ (Accessed 5.01.2020)

33 Ibid.

34 Ibid.

The Boycott

The events of the Limerick Boycott began long before 1904. Some say that there has been a small Jewish community in Ireland for perhaps a thousand years. However, the population of this community would have been quite low indeed, with only 394 recorded as living in Ireland in 1884. Due to the persecution of Jews in Europe and the pogroms in Russia, many Jews were fleeing their homes. In Ireland, this led to an influx of migrants. There were 1506 Jews in Ireland by 1891 and 3805 by 1911. Irish society treated this increase with suspicion, so much so, that formal requests were made for the police to investigate their business practices, known as 'peddling'. The accusation was that they were exploiting sections of the community by selling dodgy goods and also getting farmers into debt with the hope of securing their farms later when the farmer was unable to pay. The complaints led to an official investigation, but the police deemed the allegations as 'unfounded'[35].

At the time, Limerick was struggling economically. Also, there was still a lot of emigration of the Irish to other nations. In the sixty years leading up to 1901, the population of the province had more than halved[36]. It is accepted that the de-industrialisation of Limerick and the resulting socioeconomic factors did contribute, in part, to the Boycott of 1904[37]. However, the anti-Semitic sermons of Fr Creagh were undoubtedly the tipping point on the whole situation. Times were tight and to make it worse, the traders of Limerick now had to compete with the Jewish pedlars. Local business owners may have approached Creagh with their concerns about the pedlars bringing unwelcome competition[38]. I believe that Creagh also had other motives, which became evident over time. In his sermons, he criticised Jewish businesses and the weekly payment system, but then within a year of the boycott, he had opened a shop and offered that very same service. He had "adopted the very

---

35 Keogh, D. and McCarthy, A. (2005) 'Limerick Boycott 1904: Anti-Semitism in Ireland', Mercier Press, Cork, ISBN 1856354539, pp24.

36 Central Statistics Office (2019) 'Census through history' [online] https://www.cso.ie/en/census/censusthroughhistory/ (accessed 14.02.2019)

37 Keogh, D. and McCarthy, A. (2005) 'Limerick Boycott 1904: Anti-Semitism in Ireland', Mercier Press, Cork, ISBN 1856354539, pp31.

38 Ibid, pp34.

system for which he ordered the people to boycott the Jews"[39].

Whatever the motivations, I would suggest that Creagh's religious beliefs fostered his anti-Semitic views. In his sermon, he spoke of this saying, *"It would be madness for a man to nourish in his own breast a viper that may at any moment slay its benefactor with its poisonous view. So too, is it madness for a people to allow an evil to grow in their midst that will eventually cause them pain. Now, to what danger then did he allude tonight – what evil did he wish to direct their attention! It was that they were allowing themselves to become the slaves of Jew usurers. They knew who these were. The Jews were once the chosen people of God. God's mercy and favours towards them were boundless. They were the people of whom was born the Messiah, Jesus Christ. Our Lord and Master. But they rejected Jesus – they crucified Him – they called down the curse of His precious blood upon their own heads."* [40].

Just by examining this small section of his teaching, it reveals the spiritual blindness of Creagh. Leaders of churches should promote the Word of God and not use it to twist it and support their own flawed beliefs. He refers to Jews as being like vipers. Yes, Jesus called the Pharisees of his day vipers, not because they 'caused pain' but rather because they had injected a spiritual poison of religion into people. It was perhaps not just aimed at Pharisees, but against what the Pharisees represented, a religious person following a religious system, puffed up by pride and arrogance and yet so utterly void of love for God and love for their neighbours. Creagh's behaviour gives evidence of the same Pharasitical stance, seeking to oust the Jewish community, and spreading poison among the people.

One focus of Creagh is apportioning blame to the Jews, "*they rejected Jesus – they crucified Him*". This has been the excuse used through the centuries to persecute and kill the Jews. It is a complete lack of understanding of Jesus and His sacrifice. God had the plan made for Jesus to die on the cross before He created Adam because He knew that mankind would sin. The crucifixion was not a failure. The Jews are not the only ones responsible for Jesus having to make such a sacrifice. We all are. Every sinner is guilty, beginning with Adam and Eve and continuing with every generation. All of us have sinned. The crucifixion was a

---

39 I. Julian Grande's letter to the Times, May 1906.

40 Father Creagh (1904) 'Jewish Trading – its growth in Limerick', Munster News, Jan 13 1904.

triumph, an overwhelming display of God's love to redeem a people. All of us have rejected Jesus, all of us have crucified Him, but He has shown us His mercy by offering to pay our sin-debt in full.

Creagh was not only using his religious opinions to make a case against the Jews. He also mentions how other nations have dealt with Jews. He declared, *"They were sucking the blood of other nations, but those nations rose up and turned them out. And they came to our land to fasten themselves on us like leeches and to draw our blood when they had been forced away from other countries."* [41] . He had forgotten to mention the abusive way that the nations had been turning out the Jews. Indeed, most of the influx of Jews to Ireland was because of Russian pogroms which began after March 1881. Jews had been beaten, stoned and even killed. These refugees of racial persecution had come to Ireland to live peacefully and to make a life for themselves. They were families who had faced so much and endured. They were not 'leeches' coming to take advantage of us, but instead, they were seeking our help and protection. A chief Rabbi of London, on a visit to Dublin several years before the Boycott, *"declared that when he set foot on Irish soil, he was in the only land in Europe in which his race had never suffered persecution"* [42]. Sadly, that was about to end.

Creagh went on to say of the Jews, *"They have made Limerick their headquarters from which they can spread their rapacious nets over the country all round."*[43] This was entirely untrue. The most concentrated Jewish population was in Dublin City[44]. Creagh implied that the Jewish community planned the growth as a takeover of the country. Following that train of thought, he believed the best thing to do was to make a stand in Limerick. Many attendees at the Redemptorist church service were fired up by his words. They chose to pass by the Jewish community on their way home. One correspondent reported hearing the mob yell "down with the Jews: they kill our innocent children.[45]" The Jewish community locked up their homes and businesses, fearing the worst. The

---

41 Father Creagh (1904) 'Jewish Trading – its growth in Limerick', Munster News, Jan 13 1904.

42 Davitt, M. (1904) 'The Jews in Limerick', letter from Mr. Davitt to the editor of the Freeman, Freeman's Journal, Jan 18 1904.

43 Father Creagh (1904) 'Jewish Trading – its growth in Limerick', Munster News, Jan 13 1904.

44 The Number and Distribution of the Jewish Community in Ireland, 1891-1901, CSORP, 1905/23538, NAI.

45 Keogh, D. and McCarthy, A. (2005) 'Limerick Boycott 1904: Anti-Semitism in Ireland', Mercier Press, Cork, ISBN 1856354539, pp48.

community immediately called for police protection.

Newspapers chose to publish the full sermon. It received mixed responses from around the nation. The most ardent opposition came from Michael Davitt, who published an article to challenge Creagh. He wrote, *"The reverend gentleman...... deliberately incited the people of that city to hunt the Jews from their midst"* [46]. It was not the only opposition he received. One letter written to him stated *"you call yourself a minister of God. You are a minister of the Devil. You are a disgrace to the Catholic religion, you brute"*[47] . I think that Davitt's public opposition had shaken him. I believe this is the case because Creagh's next sermon focused mostly on giving a response back to Davitt.

However, if his first sermon was not clear enough, his following sermon *"confirmed that he was an intransigent and unrepentant anti-Semite"* [48]. One of his first points in the address was to call Davitt a traitor saying, *"I would consider myself a traitor to my religion or my country if I did not raise my voice, even though I did alone, against such an evil"*[49]. He then proceeds to take each of Davitt's points in turn and give a response. I found his second sermon to be even more shocking, Creagh also blamed the Jews as the *"cause of the Spanish inquisition"*. A sentence which seems to say that the victim is to blame for their demise. It seems so illogical, but we also see that coming through in more of his words. While claiming *"we are not persecuting them"* he also said, *"every effect has a cause"* and that *"people do not persecute their friends, but their enemies"*[50].

In my opinion, Creagh had retreated to a defensive position, offering 'evidence' from history books. He also mentioned teachings from the 16th century where Rabbis promoted killing Christians[51]. The speech also honoured 'saint' Bernard, whose actions had led to "a widespread anti-Semitic movement, which sometimes led to reprehensible

---

46 Davitt, M. (1904) 'The Jews in Limerick', letter from Mr. Davitt to the editor of the Freeman, Freeman's Journal, Jan 18 1904.

47 Holy Family Chronicles, Limerick.

48 Keogh, D. and McCarthy, A. (2005) 'Limerick Boycott 1904: Anti-Semitism in Ireland', Mercier Press, Cork, ISBN 1856354539, pp52.

49 Ibid.

50 Ibid..

51 Ibid.

excesses"[52]. Somehow Creagh completely fails to place any blame on the speaker for the violence. Can hate speech and the resulting violence be separated? I don't believe so. Creagh talked about Bernard in an attempt to remove his own guilt of inciting a mob.

He continued with more shocking statements where he reinforces his viewpoint that the Jews "were as bad an evil to Ireland as landlordism and over-taxation". He goes on to add that being slaves of the Jews "is worse than slavery to which Cromwell condemned the poor Irish who were shipped to Barbados"[53]. I find this apalling because I have read detailed accounts of that slavery to Barbados in research for a previous book. Irish people were at no point slaves to the Jews. Irish people who had spent more than they could afford had become victims to their greed and not the Jews. I think that this priest had no idea of what it meant to be a slave. Indeed, at the time of the sermons, a countless number of unmarried mothers and their children had become slaves to the Catholic religion and were beaten, abused, and raped. He stood as a representative of an institution which was guilty of slavery and pointed blame at an innocent Jewish community. The police investigation had proved their innocence. But now the police investigations are proving the guilt of Catholicism and other organisations in Ireland.

Creagh did ask the people not to harm the Jews at the end of his second sermon, but rather to boycott them. This boycott meant that Jewish traders would become unable to sell goods. Furthermore, some shops began refusing to sell to Jewish families, and their children were ostracised at school[54] . Several assaults took place, some victims made reports to the authorities, but others did not. Some pressure was put on the authorities to prosecute Creagh, but the local Inspector advised against it[55]. Those who did get charged and convicted for violence were welcomed home as heroes and paraded past the Jewish homes.

Within a year, many of the Limerick Jews had either left the city or were left destitute. I. Julian Grande, director of the Irish mission to the Jews, wrote to request help from Jews in London, saying, "I appeal to the

---

52 Article including Michael Davitt letter and Fr Creagh's second anti-Semitic speech, Limerick Echo, Jan 19, 1904.

53 Ibid.

54 Ryan, 'The Jews of Limerick', p.38.

55 Keogh, D. and McCarthy, A. (2005) 'Limerick Boycott 1904: Anti-Semitism in Ireland', Mercier Press, Cork, ISBN 1856354539, pp77.

Jews in London to assist their poor unfortunate remaining brethren and their families to leave Limerick, and let the lawless city get the reward from Him who has righteously judged Spain in the past, and its judging another semi-Christian country at present for their cruel treatment of God's ancient people"[56]. Sadly, by the end of the campaign most Limerick Jews had left for another part of Ireland.

It took almost 100 years for the Redemptorists to repent for the part that Creagh had played in these events. That event took place on 22nd November 2003, and Redemptorists from all over the world attended it. It was "alive with music and dance in the Redemptorists Church at Mount St Alphonsus last Sunday, Fr Robert McNamara while outlining the community's history in Limerick, commented how they had "badly hurt the Jews in Limerick"[57].

"It is obvious
that we can make no real contribution
to the settlement of refugees"

Frank T. Cremins[58]

56 I. Julian Grande's letter to the Times, May 1906.

57 Acheson, D. (2003) 'Fathers repent for hurting city Jews', Limerick Leader, November 29th 2003.

58 Official Report of Plenary Session of Evian Conference, July 1938.

THE EMERGENCY
CHAPTER 3

When we look back at the history of Ireland and the Jews, there are many moments of shame. But there are also positives. Jewish communities did settle here in Ireland and made lives for themselves. During the 1930s the debate of the so-called 'Jewish question' raged. It was a debate over civil, legal, national, and political status and rights of Jewish communities within nations. As the Jewish question grew in intensity, Jews in Ireland remained relatively safe from harm. Chief Rabbi Hermann Adler said this to the Irish Jews "You have come here, my foreign brethren, from a country like unto Egypt of old to a land which offers you hospitable shelter. It is said that Ireland is the only country in the world which cannot be charged with persecuting the Jews"[59]. And there were those who recognised a kinship of a shared history of persecution. Davit spoke openly of this saying "Like our own race, they have endured a persecution the records of which will for ever remain a reproach to the 'Christian' nations of Europe... we are bound in justice and in reason to all who seek the shelter of our island shores the same treatment and hospitality which the members of our own race have received at the hands of so many nations" [60].

However, some Irish people remained suspicious of the Jews, and

---

59 Quoted in Ira B. Nadel, Joyce and the Jews: Culture and Texts (University Press of Florida, Gainesville, 1996),p. 186.

60 'Ireland and the Jews', letter to the editor from Michael Davitt, Freeman's Journal , 13 July 1893.

others were outright anti-Semitic. Chaim Herzog wrote of his experience in Ireland saying, "while I did not feel outcast, I did feel indifferent" [61]. The Jewish community wanted just to be left alone to live in peace and safety[62]. Irish people had mixed views about the Jewish community. The government of De Valera in the approach of WWII reflected these opinions. Around him were both Jews and Anti-semites. Briscoe, one of the very first Jewish politicians in Ireland, set a good example for those he represented. There was a debate one day as to whether a crucifix in the Dáil would be offensive for him. He responded by saying that if it "will make you any better Christians, I certainly have no objections", and by doing so, he showed a "willingness to compromise"[63]. Another Irish official, named Bewley, was based in Germany and was often very vocal in his comments against the Jews. The government saw his behaviour at times as "an extraordinary indiscretion", and Bewley's influence over visa applications from German Jews during the 1930s was suspected to be quite negligent[64].

Ireland was refusing to address the Jewish question directly, perhaps in the hope of keeping everyone happy. The Irish stood in the middle ground through the 1920s and into the 1930s. Good leadership within the Jewish community, namely from the Herzog family proved very influential. The president of the World Zionist Organisation, Nahum Sokolow, visited Dublin in May 1933, who along with other Jewish leaders met with Eamon de Valera. "They had an hour-long interview, during which de Valera promised that the Irish Free State would use its good offices to have the issue of Jewish settlers in Palestine raised at the League of Nations"[65].

But in 1930s, we also saw the influences of European politics spreading to our shores. The Nazi Party set up offices in Ireland. Adolf Mahr "became leader of the Dublin Nazi group. According to an Irish military intelligence profile of him, Mahr was 'closely in touch with German Legation and with Nazi H.Q. in London and German Press Agency" and he conducted party meetings in a "German social club

---

61 Herzog, Living History, pp. 13-14.

62 Keogh. D. (1998) 'Jews in Twentieth-Century Ireland', Cork University Press, pp83.

63 Ibid, pp89.

64 O'Driscoll, 'Irish-German Relations', p. 26.

65 Sokolow was accompanied by his daughter, Selina. See cuttings in Nurock/Abrahamson family scrapbook in the possession of Maurice Abrahamson, Dublin.

behind the Court Laundry in Dublin" [66]. The Italian Fascist Party also met in Dublin during the 1930s. While both spread antagonism towards the Jews, neither gained momentum.

It was around this time that we saw the rise of 'blueshirtism' in Ireland. This new movement "attempted to build a coalition among the anti-Fianna Fáil parties by seeking to combine the ideologies of nationalism, Catholic corporatism and fascism"[67]. They looked to people like Pius XI and Benito Mussolini for inspiration. Beginning with the name Cumann na nGaedheal they officially launched their party at the Mansion House in Dublin. They declared that "when a Blueshirt Government is elected its first act will be to send all the foreign exploiters who have come in here during the past 12 or 13 years back to the land or lands of their birth"[68]. They would later change their name to 'Fine Gael'. When I look at their roots and where they began, then I understand better their modern-day stance regarding Israel.

We should not underestimate the negative impact that Bewley likely had as he "could exercise considerable personal authority – without reference to his superiors in Dublin – over the reception of, and advice given to, prospective Jewish refugees"[69]. Bewley, it seems had been ultimately won over by the Nazi ideology, and this came through in his reports back to Dublin about the situation and atmosphere there. For example, after attending the Nuremberg conference in 1935, he stated that Hitler was "incomparably the finest orator that I have heard"[70]. He had gone on to say that the news laws, specifically in the prohibition of 'mixed' marriages, were justified[71].

Later, the government asked Bewley to give a report on anti-Semitism in Germany which only seemed to expose his beliefs further "which uncritically mirrored the central Nazi ideas on anti-Semitism"[72]. "The Bolshevist movement in Russia, he claimed, 'was almost entirely led by Jews' ('a fact so well-known as to need no emphasis') and had been

---

66 From G2 report on Mahr, 1939, G2/0130, Irish Military Archives, Dublin.

67 Keogh, D. (1998) 'Jews in Twentieth-Century Ireland', Cork University Press, pp95-96.

68 K.C.C., 'Ireland for the Irish', Blueshirt, Jun 8 1935.

69 Keogh, D. (1998) 'Jews in Twentieth-Century Ireland', Cork University Press, pp103.

70 O'Driscoll, 'Irish-German Relations', p. 154.

71 Keogh, D. (1998) 'Jews in Twentieth-Century Ireland', Cork University Press, pp102.

72 Ibid, pp132.

'financed by American-Jewish banking houses'. He also said that 'the majority of the leaders' of the 'Communist' governments in Hungary and Bavaria after the First World War were Jews"[73]. He added "It is a notorious fact that the international white slave traffic is controlled by Jews" and "In consequence of those 'facts', Bewley said that Germany, as well as the other countries in central Europe, had 'felt obliged to eliminate the Jews from the public life of the state' with the result that 'Jews are now for practical purposes completely isolated from Germany'"[74].

In 1936 Yitzhak Herzog, an Irish Jew and good friend of De Valera, became the next chief rabbi of Palestine[75]. He had proved himself a strong leader here in Ireland and would do likewise in Palestine. Chaim Herzog recorded that De Valera frequented his father's house many times[76], a bond of friendship that would last a lifetime. The call to Israel was irresistible and the nation there was at a crucial point in history. As for Ireland, De Valera made several interventions to cut through red tape and help Jews gain visas to escape Europe and come to Ireland[77]. But until the news of the holocaust reached our shores, allowing Jews to obtain entry visas to Ireland was a political minefield.

Not only was there a considerable reluctance by Bewley in Germany, but in Ireland there was also in-house policies in State-run departments which slowed or prevented visas for Jews. We must recognise the high possibility that Jews died because of the inaction of Irish State. All of this, as aforementioned was because the Irish population itself did not view Jewish immigration in a positive light. While the Department of Justice did not record the religion of aliens applying for entry or entering the country, "in reality, the Irish authorities knew when an alien was Jewish"[78]. Therefore, they avoided addressing the issue directly but often restricted visas. Later, the news of the holocaust put pressure on Ireland to change. It was only then that the State admitted that the "immigration of Jews is generally discouraged" and that it was "the policy of the Department of Justice to restrict the

---

73 Keogh, D. (1998) 'Jews in Twentieth-Century Ireland', Cork University Press, pp133.

74 See Bewley to Walshe, Dec 9 1938, Confidential Reports, D/FA 202/63, NAI.

75 Keogh, D. (1998) 'Jews in Twentieth-Century Ireland', Cork University Press, pp110.

76 Herzog, Living History, pp. 11-12.

77 Keogh, D. (1998) 'Jews in Twentieth-Century Ireland', Cork University Press, pp127.

78 Ibid, pp128.

immigration of Jews"[79].

Robert Briscoe said that "the only solution was Palestine and the only alternative was extermination"[80]. By 1941, news of Hitler's 'Final Solution' began to leak out. Irish political leaders were undoubtedly aware of the holocaust by 1942[81]. Herzog sent a telegram to De Valera in December 1942 which said:

"REVERED FRIEND PRAY LEAVE NO STONE UNTURNED TO SAVE TORMENTED REMNANT OF ISRAEL DOOMED ALAS TO UTTER ANNIHILATION IN NAZI EUROPE GREETINGS ZIONS BLESSINGS"

The Germans seemed to have had two approaches to Ireland. Firstly, they engaged with the IRA in the hopes that Ireland would stand with Germany to fight England. The German intelligence had placed agents in Ireland which were in contact with the IRA[82]. Secondly, they made plans for a full invasion. Agents had diligently gathered extensive intelligence on Ireland during the 1930s, including detailed drawings and maps, photographs and recommended landing points on the south coast. It is also very likely that they already had all the names and addresses of all the Irish Jews[83]. It was a German "manual for invasion known as Case Green (Fall Gruen)"[84]. The Irish Jews certainly knew what could happen if Hitler's forces ever reached Ireland. Some families made plans to protect their children while others chose to enlist and do all they could to stop Germany[85].

Finally, after the revealing of the holocaust, the Irish State adopted a more liberal policy but under considerable opposition from government departments. Of course, saying we are changing is one thing, but implementing that change is something else. For example, elements of departments could easily cause delays for visas. Despite the new policy, it was still the general viewpoint that "all applications, other than applications from Jews, should be dealt with sympathetically"[86]. Even

---

79 Keogh, D. (1998) 'Jews in Twentieth-Century Ireland', Cork University Press, pp203.

80 Briscoe to Ziff, Miami Beach, Florida, Sep 22 1939, Robert Briscoe papers.

81 See document D/FA 419/44 NAI for correspondence between Jewish organisations and Dept. Foreign Affairs.

82 Keogh, D. (1998) 'Jews in Twentieth-Century Ireland', Cork University Press, pp153.

83 Ibid, pp152.

84 Ibid, pp151.

85 Ibid, pp156-8.

86 Costigan minute, Feb 7 1946, D/J 69/8027, NAI.

now, after news of the killings had reached Ireland, we were still preventing applications from Jews.

These were real people who needed Ireland's help, they were no threat to the nation, and in some cases, some had gone out of their way to help the Irish. A Jewish friend of James Joyce called Léon "helped rescue a section of Joyce's library" and "the remainder he bought back at auction". He planned to leave Paris after his son finished school term, but the Germans arrested him, and the Irish envoy was informed. They decided that "no action should be taken". "Léon, who was beaten and tortured in prison, was shot at a camp in Silesia on 4 April 1942"[87]. There were also Irish Jews who died in the holocaust. Originally it was thought that there was only one Irish Jew killed during the war, Esther Steinberg, who died in Auschwitz but new research has revealed the names of another three victims[88]. Real people, real tragedies.

A change in the Irish position, however slight, made minimal impact. Since the outbreak of war, issuing visas to Jews in Europe may have been pointless. Even getting visas for Irish citizens was difficult[89]. However, the British Foreign Office suggested that giving visas from neutral countries such as Ireland may prevent Jews from being deported to the east[90]. Getting the Germans to allow Jews to leave Germany at this stage of the war was near impossible. The German position was that "if it was intended that these families should become Irish Citizens the German authorities would... ...gladly save us the inconvenience of having so many Jews"[91]. If we were to do anything, we should have tried to do it in the 1930s when it would have been easier to do so. We had an opportunity to help the Jews, it was a "vast lost chance"[92].

Nevertheless, at this point, the Irish State did make some attempts to save Jews. One such case was when an Irish delegation attempted to save a group of Vittel Jews, of South American nationality.

---

87 Keogh, D. (1998) 'Jews in Twentieth-Century Ireland', Cork University Press, pp164

88 Burns, S. (2019) 'New research reveals three previously unknown Irish Holocaust victims' [Online] The Irish Times, https://www.irishtimes.com/news/ireland/irish-news/new-research-reveals-three-previously-unknown-irish-holocaust-victims-1.3772670 27th Jan 2019.

89 Keogh, D. (1998) 'Jews in Twentieth-Century Ireland', Cork University Press, pp180

90 Goodman to Dulanty, Sep 17 1943, D/FA 419/44, NAI.

91 Cremin to Walshe, Mar 24 1944, D/FA 419/44 NAI.

92 Keogh, D. (1998) 'Jews in Twentieth-Century Ireland', Cork University Press, pp194.

Despite their efforts in trying to cut through Irish red tape and that of Germany, news reached them that two hundred and twenty-five Vittel Jews were now in Auschwitz, Silesia. There they faced the infamous 'bath-houses' but some of them "had escaped by committing suicide"[93].

Even after the war, taking in Jewish refugees was being held back by government departments. Others rightly spoke out and so, "despite its opposition, the Department of Justice was obliged in November 1946 to reverse its decision on the admission of the Jewish orphans"[94]. Ireland issued visas for one hundred orphans on a temporary basis and housed at Clonyn Castle. Just before their arrival, someone broke into the property and attempted to set fire to it using petrol sprinkled onto the floors. Only minor damage occurred and the police at the time put it down to mere vandalism[95]. Such an act is perhaps comparable to our modern times where attacks have occurred on potential refugee properties, such as Caiseal Mara Hotel in Donegal[96] and the Shannon Key West hotel in Rooskey[97].

The Irish Jewish community provided for the needs of the children, and they soon returned to good health, before leaving to live new lives abroad in Israel, Britain, Canada, and the United States[98]. People sometimes tell the story of the assistance offered to these children and that all these children got a good life. Still, I consider it shameful for Ireland that we did not extend full visas to these children rather than just temporary help.

The government in Ireland changed but De Valera returned to power once again. Despite "those senior personnel changes, the department's 'illiberal' ethos towards the admission of aliens and refugees remained unchanged"[99], and so the "actions of the Department of Justice had, in large measure, prevented a dramatic postwar increase

---

93 Cremin to Walshe, Aug 28 1944, D/FA 419/44 NAI.

94 Keogh, D. (1998) 'Jews in Twentieth-Century Ireland', Cork University Press, pp211.

95 Eppel to Schonfeld, Mar 29 1948, Folder 1, 183/302, SS/P.

96 Maguire, 'D S. (2018) 'Donegal hotel earmarked for asylum seekers set on fire', The Irish Times, Nov 25 2018.

97 Mcdonagh M., and McMahon A. (2019 'Fire damages Rooskey hotel earmarked for asylum seekers', The Irish Times, Jan 10 2019.

98 Keogh, D. (1998) 'Jews in Twentieth-Century Ireland', Cork University Press, pp216.

99 Ibid, pp216.

in the Irish Jewish population"[100].

In the same year that the 100 children arrived in Ireland, also saw the arrival of a Nazi war criminal responsible for the death of up to one million people. Andrija Artukovic was the Ustaša Nazi minister for the interior. The Ustaša were a right-wing Catholic political group, a Nazi party. They dealt with the Jews more harshly than the German Nazis. Andrija spoke of the Jews saying they were "parasites living off the honest Croatian worker"[101]. Andrija signed racist laws and orders for concentration camps, which targeted Serbs, Jews and Roma communities, starving and poisoning people to death. His wartime Catholic links likely helped him to flee to Ireland. He arrived in July 1947 to Ireland. He later left in 1948 to the States before his eventual extradition to Yugoslavia, trial and death sentence.

This arrival of a war criminal was not just a once off occurrence, many prominent Nazi leaders came to either live in Ireland or to use it as a base until they could secure a visa to another country, usually outside Europe. Strangely, once they were here "these Nazi collaborators penetrated every level of Irish society"[102]. The Irish openness to take in ex-Nazis "baffled the allies"[103]. What frustrates me is that Ireland seemed to give a greater welcome to Nazis than returning war veterans! An RTE documentary discussed in detail some of those who came to Ireland:

a) Célestin Lainé was a commander in the Bretton SS Militia who arrived in Ireland in December 1947. He was a Bretton, born in Brittany and was inspired by the IRA who secured independence by violence. The Germans used the group as militia and tasked them with finding resistance fighters. There are many mass graves in Brittany attributed to them.
b) Pieter Menten arrived in Ireland in Feb 1963. In the 1980s, it came to light that he was a war criminal. Irish people treated him as a "Dutch businessman" and a "retired millionaire art collector"[104]. Menten lost money and property when Russia invaded, so he went out and looted from wealthy Jews — using

---

100 Keogh, D. (1998) 'Jews in Twentieth-Century Ireland', Cork University Press, pp223.

101 Ireland's Nazis (2007) Tile Films, Episode One.

102 Ireland's Nazis (2007) Tile Films, Episode Two.

103 Ireland's Nazis (2007) Tile Films, Episode One.

104 Ibid.

a SS uniform and title to commit murder. Investigators uncovered a mass grave and gathered enough evidence to press charges.

c) Helmut Clissman was an Abwehr Intelligent Agent arrived in June 1948. He was the chief expert on Ireland. He came as a student in the 1930s and became involved with the Irish Nazi Party and the IRA. He arranged for the release of Frank Ryan, who was in a Spanish prison. He was then recalled to Germany and worked in the German foreign ministry, then special operations and German intelligence to help make invasion plans of Ireland. He suffered torture in a camp after the war. He later became an early member of Amnesty International.

d) Albert Folens was a member of the Flemish SS, and he arrived in Ireland in October 1948 where he established a successful publishing company. To this day, "questions remain unanswered about the wartime career of Ireland's leading educational publisher"[105]. Although he never saw front line action, he did work with the secret service. After the war, he was tried for treason in Belgium and convicted for ten years. He had only served two years when he escaped. He used a well-known escape route from Belgium to the Netherlands through a monastery that was on the border and then flew from Amsterdam to Liverpool and later on to Dublin.

e) Albert Luykx was a member of the Black Brigade, a businessman and a Flemish nationalist. A court gave him a death penalty after the war. He escaped and fled to Ireland. Once there, he established a successful restaurant in Sutton. He got involved with Fianna Fáil but got embroidered with scandal in 1970 after a botched attempt at smuggling guns for the IRA. They sent Luykx to obtain weapons because he spoke German, but a lack of know-how in exporting, he failed. Newspapers later called him a "naive fool"[106].

f) Otto 'Scarface' Skorzeny was part of the Waffen SS Commandos and arrived in Ireland in May 1959. People once dubbed him 'the most dangerous man in Europe'. There was a concern that he might use Ireland as a base for NeoNazism and so the "Irish government were worried about why he would want to come

---

105 Ireland's Nazis (2007) Tile Films, Episode Two.

106 Ibid.

and live in this country"[107]. He saw action against Russia and became a Nazi hero. He led the mission to rescue Mussolini. Hitler put him in charge of rounding up those who failed in an assassination attempt in 1944. After the war, the Allies put him on trial for war crimes, but he later escaped.

One of the most positive steps that Ireland did make was regarding the constitution put forward by De Valera in 1939. Under a particular clause, Jewish citizens of Ireland were given equal rights and so at the time, Irish Jews were "probably the only Jewish community in the world to be constitutionally protected in this explicit manner. In practice, too, the Jews of Ireland have always felt free from discrimination. In fact, Ireland is one of the very few countries that has never blemished its record by any serious anti-Jewish outrages"[108]. Later, De Valera "shocked Irish people and outraged the leaders of the Allied powers by visiting the German minister in Dublin, Edouard Hempel, on 2 May to express his condolences on the death of Adolf Hitler"[109]. In 1959, De Valera retired from party political life and then became President of Ireland later that year.

Ireland gave de facto recognition of Israel in 1949 and then changed to de jure recognition in 1963. In 1966, Irish Jews donated a forest of 10,000 trees at Kfar Kana and named it after De Valera. The Jewish community recognised his efforts in the "cause of peace and freedom", he had "evinced understanding and sympathy towards the restoration of Israel in the land of its fathers"[110]. Herzog had been "deeply moved by his understanding of the spiritual motive of Israel reborn"[111]. An exchange of diplomatic representatives happened later in December 1974. An Israeli diplomat Max Nurock once stated that "Designations of Irish tribes and princes strangely echo the syllables in the names of the great figures of the Bible's Book of Genesis. The stone of Tara is claimed to be that whereon the patriarch Jacob reclined in his famous

107 Ireland's Nazis (2007) Tile Films, Episode Two.

108 Jakobovits, Journal of a Rabbi, p.64.

109 Keogh, D. (1998) 'Jews in Twentieth-Century Ireland', Cork University Press, pp199.

110 Herzog to Abrahamson, Aug 18 1966, File 844, Eamon de Valera papers, Franciscan Archives, Killiney, Co. Dublin.

111 Ibid.

slumber"[112].

There was still a significant influence in Irish society by the Catholic church, so when Pope Paul VI and over 2000 bishops put their signatures to the 'Nostra Aetate' in 1965, it was bound to have an impact in Ireland but also around the world. *Nostra Aetate* repudiated and deplored 'all hatreds, persecutions and displays of anti-Semitism directed against Jews at any time and from any source"[113]. However, anti-Semitism was still lingering in Ireland in the 1970s. A survey carried out in 1978 revealed trends such as (a) 75% agreed that the Jews were responsible for the crucifixion of Jesus, and (b) 57% believed that Jewish wealth was out of proportion to the number of Jews[114]. A later study in 1996 showed "a relatively high level of prejudice towards Jews in the more rural areas of Ireland"[115].

"There has never been any official expression
of regret from any Irish government
at the State's refusal to admit
into Ireland the many Jews
fleeing from Nazi terror"
Alan Shatter, Fine Gael TD

112 Max Nurock speech, Aug 18 1966, File 844, Eamon de Valera papers, Franciscan Archives, Killiney, Co. Dublin.

113 Keogh, D. (1998) 'Jews in Twentieth-Century Ireland', Cork University Press, pp236.

114 Micheal Mac Greil, Prejudice and Tolerance in Ireland: Based on a Survey of Intergroup Attitudes of Dublin Adults and Other Sources (no publisher listed, 1978), p. 525.

115 Keogh, D. (1998) 'Jews in Twentieth-Century Ireland', Cork University Press, pp237.

NUREMBERG
CHAPTER 4

The Lord has led me to travel to Germany on two previous occasions, both unrelated. However, I had a distinct feeling that my need to go to Nuremberg had a connection to the more recent trip. I had travelled to Berlin in 2017 at the culmination of the intercessory mission to defy witchcraft powers in Europe and the stronghold they had held over Ireland. In my preparation for that journey, I had understandably done a lot of research. One particular location which was of interest to me was the Pergamon Altar which is on display in a museum in Berlin. However, just before I travelled, I heard that the Altar was not open to the public at that time due to renovations in that part of the museum. On that occasion, I just took it that the Lord didn't want me to see it – and it did help me to focus on what the Lord did want me to see. But I did go to the museum to visit the gates (Babylon gate and the Miletus Gate) and raise a banner for the Lord. When I arrived, I learnt of another vital site that I must squeeze into my trip. If the Pergamon Altar had of been open, it might have used up my time and focus which were undoubtedly needed elsewhere.

From my research about the Altar, I knew it originated from Pergamon and that Hitler used a replica of it to stand on and give speeches. I had assumed that the replica altar had been in Berlin and destroyed during or after the war. It was not until I began the research for this intercessory mission and the persecution of the Jews that I came across the information that Hitler's replica altar was at Nuremberg and that it still exists. Once I realised this, I knew that perhaps I was never meant to go to the Pergamon Altar (and face what it represented in its original form) but instead stand against its modern application in the time of the Nazis.

As I began to make plans to go to Germany, a couple of things occurred. First, someone gave me an old autoharp. It had faded paint, split wood, broken strings and rusted metal. Initially, I just saw it as a restoration project, but when I researched its history, I found out that craftsmen had made it at the Hopf factory in Nördlingen, Germany. I began to see the gift as something more significant. Secondly, my wife and I had been part of an intercessory team supporting a mission covering the island of Ireland in 2019, all 32 counties. The autoharp has 32 strings, and so each string can represent a county. As I stripped the instrument down, I decided to replace the backboard (or foundation of the autoharp). Just like in Ireland, and perhaps Germany, we need a better foundation – that of Jesus. Secondly, after sharing briefly on social media that I will be travelling to Germany, I was contacted by an intercessor. They shared with me about a link between Ireland, Germany, and Israel. For me, the call was confirmation for me.

"You shall say, 'Hear the word of the Lord, O kings of Judah and inhabitants of Jerusalem. Thus says the Lord of hosts, the God of Israel: Behold, I am bringing such disaster upon this place that the ears of everyone who hears of it will tingle." Jeremiah 19:3 ESV

In preparation for the trip, I set aside some time to prepare and to do some research and what I found amazed me. I discovered that Irish people had been to Nuremberg during Hitler's rule and at crucial points in history. Indeed, at least some Irish people had attended the 1929, 1934 and 1935 Nazi Party rallies and perhaps the others too. Previously I have mentioned **Charles Bewley**, who served as Ireland's minister to Berlin between 1933 and 1939. He had been responsible for hindering visa applications made by Jews. He was also an outspoken anti-Semite. It is perhaps no surprise that he attended the Nuremberg Rallies. I was unable to find out how many he attended, but he was certainly there for the 1935 Rally, which was when Hitler enacted the 'Nuremberg Laws'. It was after this rally that he had called Hitler the greatest orator he had ever seen.

The next discovery I came across was the story of **Michael Keogh**. Michael was from the village of Tullow. As a teen, he left for America where he joined the IRB group Clan Na Gael. In 1913, Michael joined the Royal Irish Regiment but got into trouble for his republican ideals. He fought in the trenches of WWI until he ended up in a German POW camp. After that, Michael switched sides and eventually joined the German army and rose to the rank of Field Lieutenant.

From May 1919, he was serving as a duty officer in Munich. One night while on patrol he was alerted to a riot where he saw around two-hundred men beating up two men, and he saw that bayonets were about to be used on them. Michael ordered his men to fire a warning shot and then dragged the two victims off to safety. Michael recalled "The fellow with the moustache gave his name as Adolf Hitler"[116]. Later that year, Michael returned to Ireland and assisted Michael Collins in trafficking guns between Germany and Ireland. A decade later, he returned to live in Germany and worked as an engineer in Berlin. He was in Nuremberg in 1930 and attended the rally there[117] which was just before Hitler gained power. In 1934, things took a turn for the worst. First, he believed that he had become a 'marked man' after a Hitler youth attacked his son, and he had written a letter of complaint to Goebbels. Then secondly on the infamous 'Night of the Long Knives', he had come very close to have been spotted by the SS and killed. Michael and his family left Germany on 8 Sep 1936.

The next story begins with a Dublin born girl called **Bridget Dowling**. As a seventeen-year-old, she went with her father to the Dublin Horse show in 1909. Her father had got talking with a foreign businessman called Alois, who was on a trip to Ireland. Alois and Bridget fell deeply in love, and they eloped to London and were wed[118]. Alois Hitler was Adolf's eldest brother. Alois and Bridget moved to Liverpool and set up a business. Bridget claimed that Adolf visited them there, but this has been unverified. Sometime after Bridget and Alois had a son, Alois fled England for Germany and left behind his debts and his wife and child. He re-joined the German army, and Bridget received a fake letter informing her of his death. Many years later, she heard from Alois again,

---

116 Corless, D. (2011) 'The Irish man who saved Hitler' [Online] The Independant, https://www.independent.ie/lifestyle/the-irish-man-who-saved-hitler-26713584.html March 15 2011.

117 Irish Brigade [Online] http://www.irishbrigade.eu/recruits/kehoe-michael.html

118 Hoyes, F. (2015) 'The strange tale of the Irish Hitlers – the connection between Bridget Hitler and the Nazi leader' [Online] Irish Central https://www.irishcentral.com/roots/the-irish-hitler-the-strange-tale-of-bridget-hitler-and-the-nazi-leader-156889665-237617891 Dec 27 2015.

and he was asking for his son Patrick to come to Germany to visit. Patrick went to Germany, and his father introduced him to his famous uncle at the 1929 Nuremberg Rally. Initially, Patrick welcomed his uncle in helping him find a job, but the relationship between them soured. Patrick later told audiences that his uncle was a "madman surrounded by the worst types of men"[119]. Patrick returned to his mother, and then they immigrated to the US and changed their names. Patrick later enlisted and went to fight in the army against Germany and his uncle.

The next person of note is a man called **Nicolas Tindall** who served with the Royal Air Force. He became a prisoner of war in 1940 after crash landing in France. He was assigned to the POW camp called 'Stalag Luft III' where he became involved in digging three tunnels named Tom, Dick and Harry. It was the camp of the infamous 'Great Escape' – a plan for 200 officers to escape. As they prepared the tunnels, those involved were in fear of being discovered. Roger Bushell approached Nicolas to ask him to check if a fellow Irishman was an informant. Nicolas later gave feedback that the man would never inform – information that saved that man's life. The movie about the 'Great Escape' portrays it as a somewhat success. In reality, 50 of the 75 escapee officers were shot dead, mostly after being captured – Hitler himself had requested their termination. Nicolas's story gets caught up with Nuremberg because in January 1945, due to the approaching Red Army, Stalag Luft III was evacuated and the prisoners marched westwards. Nicolas recounted walking in freezing conditions as "one of his worst experiences"[120]. The Germans evacuated the prisoners from this camp to Stalag Luft XIII-D, which was the POW camp built on the Nuremberg Rally grounds[121].

I feel that in Ireland, we often think that we were somewhat separate from what happened in WWII. That we did not partake of Hitler's evil, nor were we victims. That assumption is just wrong. One group of Irish men who got caught up in the war were a group of 32 Irish merchant seamen who served in the Merchant Navy. They had set sail

---

119 Hayes, F. (2015) 'The strange tale of the Irish Hitlers – the connection between Bridget Hitler and the Nazi leader' [Online] Irish Central https://www.irishcentral.com/roots/the-irish-hitler-the-strange-tale-of-bridget-hitler-and-the-nazi-leader-156889665-237617891 Dec 27 2015.

120 The Irish Times (2006) 'Irishman who helped dig tunnels for the Great Escape' [Online] https://www.irishtimes.com/news/irishman-who-helped-dig-tunnels-for-the-great-escape-1.1017618 Feb 18 2006.

121 Wikipedia (2019) 'Stalag XIII-D' [Online] https://en.m.wikipedia.org/wiki/Stalag_XIII-D

from South Africa and were on route to India when they were intercepted off the coast of Madagascar. They were initially brought to Bordeaux and then the Germans sent them on to Drancy concentration camp and tried to convince them to join the German military intelligence, but they refused. So, they were instead sent to Sandbostel work camp in northern Germany and then on to Milag Nord camp in 1941. Their captors continually pressurised them to join the German side. They were given the carrot, moved to Bremen where they had greater freedom and rations, but that didn't entice them. They were then given the stick and transferred to Bremen-Farge camp to be tortured by the SS.

They had now entered a slave labour camp. They had a 12-hour working day, often in freezing temperatures as low as minus 20 degrees. Life expectancy was so small amongst the workers from this camp that their workgroups were nicknamed 'suicide squads'[122]. Five of the men died at the camp. The others survived and returned to Ireland after their release at the end of the war. Some returned to Germany (Hamburg)[123] to give testimony at war criminal trials as to the brutality of their treatment. Christopher Ryan, who spent most of the next eight years in hospital, was one of those who returned to give evidence. These men had pleaded to the Irish official in Berlin to ask for him to secure their release – the government did nothing. When these men went to give evidence at the trials, the Irish State did not support them. In fact, "our government was actively opposed to such trials, and lobbied vigorously against them"[124].

James Brady and Frank Stringer who served with the Royal Irish Fusiliers were captured in 1940 and ended up at Camp Friesack, a camp used by the Germans for Irish soldiers that they wished to turn to their side[125]. Trying to convince the Irish to collaborate seemed a common tactic of the Germans. These two men signed up with the SS and ended up in the special force's unit alongside Hitler's top soldier Otto Skorzeny.

---

122 The Independent (2012) 'irish slaves of the nazis remembered' [Online] https://www.independent.ie/lifestyle/irish-slaves-of-the-nazis-remembered-28942912.html

123 Farrell, S. (2013) 'The lost story of our Nazi slaves' [Online] The Independent https://www.independent.ie/entertainment/the-lost-story-of-our-nazi-slaves-29074902.html Feb 17 2013.

124 The Independent (2012) 'irish slaves of the nazis remembered' [Online] https://www.independent.ie/lifestyle/irish-slaves-of-the-nazis-remembered-28942912.html

125 Pettit, C. (2017) 'The Strange Tale of Two Irishmen Who Fought for Hitler' [Online] Ozy, https://www.ozy.com/flashback/the-strange-tale-of-two-irishmen-who-fought-for-hitler/78944 Jul 3 2017.

There were perhaps not the only ones to collaborate. It is important to note that they had become part of the SS. At the Nuremberg Rallies, all new units of the SS would undergo a ritual with a flag. The 'Blutfahne' was a flag covered with the blood of Andreas Bauriedl (a martyr killed by Munich police). This flag became the 'sacred' symbol of the Nazi movement, and at the Nuremberg rallies, the SS would touch their flags against it to 'sanctify them'. I believe that anyone who served in the SS entered into a blood covenant.

Looking at these examples, and they are just a sample of what happened during the war, Ireland got to experience Hitler and Nazi oppression and corruption. We had those who helped, others who sought gain, some who collaborated, others that died, and even Irish slaves who afterwards went to help bring justice.

The history of Nuremberg is quite an interesting one. It was once an Imperial city and the location of an imperial castle in 1050. It was the 'unofficial capital' of the Holy Roman Empire, perhaps because of the Imperial Diet (or Reichstag) and also the courts which met at the castle[126]. A massacre of Jews happened here in both 1298 and 1349. Hundreds were burnt at the stake or expelled from the city. In 1356, Charles IV's 'Golden Bull' named Nuremberg as the location where elected kings must hold their initial Imperial Diet. In the 15th and 16th Centuries, Nuremberg became the centre of Germany's Renaissance movement. Also, Protestants and Catholics signed a peace treaty in the city in 1532.

Perhaps, the history of Nuremberg is why Hitler chose to use it as the spiritual centre of the Nazis. People using ancient places for new purposes is not an alien concept in Ireland. The church often convened synods in Ireland at Clonmacnoise – despite it being a ruin, just to use the sense of authority that the name carries. The Reichstag was the '1st Reich' and Hitler was establishing the 3rd Reich, the third Reichstag. So, Nuremberg was the centre, the heart of the Nazi movement in many ways:

- During the war, the city became the headquarters of Wehrkreis (military district) XIII, and an important site for military production, including aircraft, submarines, and tank engines.
- In 1938, Hitler received the 'imperial regalia' used during the first empire that included a sword.

---

126 Wikipedia (2019) 'Nuremberg' [Online] https://en.wikipedia.org/wiki/Nuremberg.

- The Nazis held Nuremberg Rallies at Zeppelinfeld.
- Nuremberg was the home of Julius Streicher whose publications were a central element of the Nazi propaganda machine.
- Hitler ordered the building of Kongresshalle to have 50,000 seats and house congress meetings.
- Märzfeld was a parade ground, relating to the Roman god of war – Mars (March in German) and was used in March 1935 to re-establish the authority of the Reich.
- Hitler laid the foundation stone of the Deutsches Stadion in 1937 – a stadium that would have seated 400,000 – excavations began but were never completed. The site of the pit is now filled with water and called Silbersee.
- They constructed the Great Road, which ran from Kongresshalle to the Märzfeld and pointed towards the Imperial Castle. It linked the First Reich to the Third.
- Ehrenhall or 'Hall of Honour' was a hall with an arched front which faced a cobbled stone terrace, which had pylons on either side of it, seven on each side which held 14 fire pits (last lit at 1938 rally). It was here that Nazis enacted the very first 'cult of the dead' ceremony. Facing this was a grandstand which could seat 500 dignitaries called the 'Ehrentribüne' – the very first Nazi building in Nuremberg.

The Nazi Rallies in Nuremberg grew in strength each time and usually had a 'theme'. They weren't just a rally lasting a couple of hours like what we would see in modern politics. They would last anywhere from a day up to a week. They continued annually until the beginning of WWII. Ironically the war began the day before a planned rally which would have been called the 'rally of peace'. These rallies were more than just a political event. Gatherings included speeches, marching and ceremonies. The following page displays a list of the annual events, their dates, themes and also other relevant information.

1	27 Jan 1923	Munich	The First Party Congress	
2	1-2 Sep 1923	Nuremberg	'German day rally'	
3	3-4 Jul 1926	Weimar	'Refounding Congress'	
4	19-21 Aug 1927	Nuremberg	'Day of Awakening'	
5	1-4 Aug 1929	Nuremberg	'Day of Composure'	Created propaganda movie Der Nürnberger Parteitag der NSDAP
6	30 Aug -3 Sep 1933	Nuremberg	'Rally of Victory'	Created propaganda movie Der Sieg des Glaubens
7	5-10 Sep 1934	Nuremberg	'Rally of Unity and Strength'	700,000 attended. 152 searchlights created the 'cathedral of light'
8	10-16 Sep 1935	Nuremberg	'Rally of Freedom'	Declared freedom from Versailles, reinstated military service and introduced the Nuremberg Laws
9	8-14 Sep 1936	Nuremberg	'Rally of Honour'	Footage used for movie Festliches Nürnberg. Remilitarization of Rhineland.
10	6-13 Sep 1937	Nuremberg	'Rally of Labour'	Footage used for movie Festliches Nürnberg. Celebrated reduction in unemployment.
11	5-12 Sep 1938	Nuremberg	'Rally of Greater Germany'	Austria annexed.
12	2-11 Sep 1939	Nuremberg	'Rally of Peace'	Cancelled as Germany invaded Poland on 1st September, and ignited WWII.

After the war, the Allies chose Nuremberg as the location where trials against many prominent Nazis would take place. Other war crime trials would follow. They were a series of tribunals held by the Allied Forces to prosecute people from all aspects of the Nazi war machine. This initial trial at Nuremberg tried 24 men and hearings occurred between 1945 and 1946. The Palace of Justice was chosen as the location because it was mostly undamaged, and the Allies thought it fitting to bring justice back to where injustice had perhaps begun. The judges sentenced twelve men to death, but only 10 made it to the gallows. There were 13 steps and 13 nooses. The execution was botched, and the noose failed to break their necks, and so they took a prolonged time to hang. The bodies were incinerated and scattered into the river Isar, a tributary of the Danube. Strangely, just as Nuremberg trials and prosecution finished, the 'Iron Curtain' speech was given.

Mission Trip - Nurnberg, September 2019

I had arranged for a short trip to Nuremberg. Initially, I had just intended to visit Hitler's podium at Zeppelin Field. But as I prepared and prayed, I began to realise that it would be more than that, and so it would be a very tight timeline. I would need to ensure I did not get distracted by the time element while at various sites, to ensure I didn't miss anything that the Lord had sent me to do. I had not been out of Ireland since 2017, a year in which I had travelled to several European countries, including Germany. I was feeling a bit rusty, but I did feel as prepared as I could be.

On Saturday 13th September I got up at 5am and left for the airport. I was already tired, having been out on a late house call to a friend that Thursday. I was praying as soon as I left the house and praying until I reached the airport. I prayed that I would not have to have a long queue at security, and surprisingly I went straight through security, which if you have ever been to Dublin airport, you will know is a miracle. I think the Lord was letting me know that I was stepping into His perfect timing for the weekend.

As I walked to the boarding gate, I felt an incredible presence of the Holy Spirit with me and speaking to me about a few things. When the call went out for boarding, I went and stood in the non-priority queue, but the Lord somehow moved me to the front. I watched as the priority queue was showing their ID and boarding pass and walking through the gate. The machine made two beeping sounds. Then I watched as one man stepped up and the machine made only one beep. The computer had frozen, and everything ground to a halt. I began praying about it. About ten minutes later, we were permitted to board via a manual boarding method. I found out then on my return to Ireland that a system-wide crash had just occurred, and flights across Europe had been grounded or delayed[127]. As for me, I was in the Lord's hands and on my plane on my way to Frankfurt.

I arrived in Frankfurt, a little late, but safely and I was content. I would have to wait a fair while for my luggage. As I sat there, I reflected on the fact that in 1934, from Frankfurt, one could see the 'Cathedral of Light' shining into the sky at Nuremberg. The two cities are about 140 miles away from each other! I walked out of the airport and into the train station where I bought a high-speed train to Nuremberg. I sat down next to a man and got talking with him. He was studying for his doctorate in Egyptology. I think he was cheating in a way, as he is from Egypt. A fascinating chat which was developing towards me sharing my faith, but we were interrupted by a lady who wanted her 'reserved seat'. It was his seat, so I gave him mine and found myself another chair nearby. As I sat down on a nearby chair, the girl next to me said that I would need to give up the place at the next stop. She pointed up to a reserved message. I just prayed, and within a few minutes, the digital 'reserved' message disappeared.

Due to the delay, I decided that I should go first to my accommodation, drop off the suitcase and then head back out. I arrived at the hotel simultaneously to a couple who were on the train near me. Between the three of us, we managed to figure out how to get the key from the key box. I was soon back on the U1 train back to the central station. During the day, the Lord highlighted several people that I then talked with to share my testimony about what God had done for me.

My first stop was going to be Hersbruck where I was expecting to find a memorial of a Nazi work camp there. Hersbruck was a satellite camp of Flossenbürg concentration camp. The workers were to be used to excavate an underground factory for BMW aircraft engines[128]. The prisoners were also used to provide a service to Nuremberg, helping to rebuild it after Allied bombings to get unexploded munitions from buildings and so on. The camp opened on 17th May 1944, and it was in operation for about eleven months in which time some 4000 of the 9000

---

127 Brown, F. (2019) 'Ryanair flights grounded across Europe after 'major system failure'' [Online] The Metro https://metro.co.uk/2019/09/14/ryanair-flights-grounded-across-europe-major-systems-failure-10741748/ Sep 14 2019.

128 Memorial Museums [Online] 'Dokumentationsstätte KZ Hersbruck' https://www.memorialmuseums.org/staettens/druck/1190

prisoners died[129]. I had heard about concentration camps, but never about Nazi work camps. The work camps provided slave labour to keep the war machine going. Therefore, many industrialists were involved. Many German companies were once Nazi collaborators and used slave labour in their factories. They worked the people to death. The list of collaborating companies included BMW, Audi, Opel, Ford, Porsche, Nestle, Allianz, IBM, Siemens and many more[130] [131]. The Allies charged some industrialists immediately following the war. None were convicted. The Allies instead chose to use them to help rebuild Germany and Europe.

I think that I wanted to visit the site because I was on a journey to understand the wrongs done between brothers and to learn more about the wrongs done to the Jews during the war. Secondly, I knew that at least some Irish people had ended up as slaves at similar camps. These work camps were in place all over Germany and their occupied territories. There were over 15,000 camps in Germany alone[132].

At the central station, I caught a train heading for Hersbruck. I soon realised that I might have got on the wrong one. It was a local train rather than a national train – a journey not covered by my ticket. I ended up talking to a lady about it, asking her about the train destination. It was to go to Hersbruck, just a lot more stops. It was taking a long time, and then when I arrived, I realised that there were two train stations in the town, and I had arrived at the one which was further from the mission site. I faced a long walk, and for a few reasons, I had developed a headache. With all of this, I was struggling. It was a beautiful day, but night-time was approaching, and perhaps I was a little stressed about getting there and praying before darkness.

When I arrived at the location, it was not as I expected. There was an information centre there, set up to show a projected video, but it was not operational. I went and sat in the rose garden. I was tired,

---

129 Memorial Museums [Online] 'Dokumentationsstätte KZ Hersbruck' https://www.memorialmuseums.org/staettens/druck/1190

130 Wikipedia (2019) 'List of companies involved in the Holocaust' [Online] https://en.wikipedia.org/wiki/List_of_companies_involved_in_the_Holocaust

131 Paoletti, G. (2017) '7 Major Brands That Were Once Nazi Collaborators' [Online] https://allthatsinteresting.com/major-brands-nazi-collaborators

132 Ferree, C. (2019) 'Full listing of concentration camps' [Online] https://www.jewishvirtuallibrary.org/full-listing-of-concentration-camps#germ

overheated, and so I struggled to pray at all, let alone to 'hear' part of a song the Lord wanted me to learn. It was too much, and when I left, I felt depleted.

I returned to Nuremberg, along the correct train route. There I got some refreshments first to try and shake off the headache. I had also contacted home for prayer support regarding the same issue. I had several places which I felt I should visit and had options, but I decided to go to the Imperial Castle. I walked through the centre of the town. It reminded me of Basel as it had a similar feel to the city. It was the height of summer, and there were many tourists around as well as locals enjoying the pleasant weather. The city was quite beautiful. Then, while trying to get to the castle, I got lost, or did I? I took a wrong turn and ended up going into a tunnel which went through the Castle wall. I was within the ancient wall.

A busker was playing the guitar, and the sound of his music was echoing through the tunnel. I noticed what I thought to be an Irish twang to it, but it was not until I passed by the man that he put down his guitar and began to play an Irish song on a tin whistle. I turned and walked back to where he was and sat down in the tunnel near to him and listened. After he finished playing a few tunes, he paused for a few minutes and so I talked to him. He was half Irish, half South African. He had spent some time on the Aran Islands where had been taught to play the tin whistle by one of Ireland's most prominent musicians. He now lived in Germany. He shared about his journey in Ireland, and I shared about why I had come to Nuremberg. After that, he shook my hand, and we went our separate ways. I felt like he had welcomed me to the nation. As soon as this happened, the atmosphere changed, and it broke the spiritual resistance that I had been feeling. The headache was also gone. I continued up to the castle overlooking Nuremberg and then went back to the hotel for the night.

In the morning, I got up and packed my bags and got going. This last day was the main event. I was heading to the Nuremberg rally grounds. It was a challenging walk across to Zeppelin Field, estimated to take about forty minutes, but I was quite tired from the day before which slowed me down. Between the tiredness and a flawed map, navigation was frustrating. As soon as I reached the park, I began to feel like I was being followed. I kept moving and prayed for the Lord's protection. Starting at the hotel, I had noticed several piles of wood stacked up and saw many more stacks in the park itself. I felt like the Lord was highlighting it to me. It made me think of the verses that say that branches that do not bear fruit will be cut off and then thrown in the fire.

I also noticed a load of birch trees in one area of the park. Birch trees have been nicknamed 'weeping trees'. I thought about the weeping that flowed because of the actions which took place here many years ago. I reached the first lake, which was now on my left as I walked. I passed by this lake and then to the next, from where I could see the Nazi U-shaped building across the water. Soon, I caught my first glimpse of the Zeppelin field as I approached it from the side. The side sections were fenced off, and access restricted. So, I was relieved to see that officials had not fenced off the podium. A local football club was using much of the field as a training ground. Also, a road now passed right by podium.

I began to climb the steps and stopped when I noticed a door lower down which had 'damen' on it, but I am not sure what this represented. I continued up onto the podium. This place was where Hitler made his speeches to the people of Germany. I sat down and began to pray. I prayed about all the Irishmen who had been in Nuremberg and about the various reasons why they were. I asked the Lord if he would set my people free from the evil that they participated with, and if He would forgive us for our foolish actions, and lack of effort.

Lord, let Your Righteousness reign,

Let it reign over me

Over my family,

My nation and my people[133].

Then I took out my German autoharp and played a song, releasing a sound of freedom.

From there, I headed to the War Memorial, where I also sought the Lord in prayer and worship. I played a song with my autoharp, and then I took out my Low-D tin whistle, and the sound echoed through the arches and then out across the park.

After I had finished praying, the Lord asked me to turn to a verse from Jeremiah which read *"'Shall I not punish them for these things?' Says the Lord 'And shall I not avenge Myself on such a nation as this?'* Jer 5:9

133 See Isaiah 32:1

ESV.

This answer was not what I had expected when I had been asking for forgiveness for Ireland. So, I asked the Lord in response, 'What if my people, every county, would take the Father's heart and seek You, will You then forgive us and heal our land?'

There was a man there at the memorial, perhaps an agent of the enemy. Afterwards, he followed me to the tram station and sat down next to me. I began to pray for protection, and he began to twitch. He tried to say something, but he couldn't. Then he stood up and went out of sight around the side of the station and began to have a conversation with himself and made weird noises. I was very grateful to the Lord for protection. The one thing I sensed from this man was a danger.

"In former days when the great Famine and other disasters lay heavy on this land, many of our people sought and received the hospitality of other countries. Let us now show that we, too, can be generous and prove to the world that the Irish people believe that Christians of whatever race or blood are sons of the same Father Whose brotherhood is shown, above all, in this, that 'they love one another'"

The Irish Co-Ordinating Committee for the Relief of Christian Refugees from Central Europe, 1938

GENTILE SOJOURNERS
CHAPTER 5

"Afterward the children of Israel shall return
and seek the Lord their God,
and David their king,
and they shall come in fear to the Lord
and to his goodness in the latter days" Hosea 3:5 ESV

There were two classifications of sojourners in ancient Israel. Some of these people had become resident in the land, but others were there temporarily. As all the property belonged to the Israelites, they would have had an inferior place in society. Most of them were poor, but some were wealthy[134]. They were permitted to share the gleanings of the harvest and the fallen fruit in the vineyard[135]. The word 'toshab'[136] is translated and defined as 'a sojourner'[137] meaning a foreign resident, a settler, or a tenant and originates from the word 'yashab'[138]. 'Yashab' is the verb to dwell, so such sojourners were not Israelites, but they lived and remained in the land.

---

134 See Leviticus 25:47.

135 See Leviticus 19:10 & 23:22.

136 Occurs 14 times.

137 Strong, James (1890), 'The Exhaustive Concordance of the Bible', Cincinnati: Jennings & Graham,reference 8453.

138 Thomas, R. (1981) 'NAS Exhaustive Concordance', Broadman & Holman Publishers.

The second word for sojourner is 'ger'[139] [140] meaning an alien, foreigner, immigrant or a stranger and originates from the word 'guwr'[141]. The term 'guwr' refers to newcomers who had come to dwell in the land (definite or indefinitely) without original rights. This use of this word might also have included the earlier inhabitants of Canaan as not all of them were slain as commanded nor forced into slavery[142]. 'Guwr' would also have been used to categorize those who had come to seek refuge in times of famine and drought, or even to flee invading armies[143].

Over time the sojourners became intermixed, both culturally and religiously. They were subject to religious laws such as those regarding ritual purification, incest, food. They obeyed the Sabbath[144] and took part in religious festivals, including fasting and offering burnt sacrifices. If circumcised, they could even sacrifice the paschal lamb[145]. But there were perhaps further complications as third-generation Edomites and Egyptians could be admitted to the congregation of the Lord[146]. Ammonites and Moabites could join after the tenth generation[147]. At the time of Ezra and Nehemiah, Israel-Palestine marriages were deemed illegitimate because of the laws[148] but Israel absorbed other foreigners as long as they converted. The conversion of the Gentiles is alluded to by the prophets, especially Isaiah and Zechariah.

There are two Greek words used in the bible to refer to Gentiles. The first is 'ethnos' meaning 'a race, a nation, the nations (as distinct from Israel)[149] and is very similar in meaning to the Hebrew word 'goy'[150]. The

---

139 Occurs 92 times.

140 Strong, James (1890), 'The Exhaustive Concordance of the Bible', Cincinnati: Jennings & Graham, reference 1616

141 Thomas, R. (1981) 'NAS Exhaustive Concordance', Broadman & Holman Publishers.

142 See Deuteronomy 7:2, 1 Kings 5:29, 2 Chronicles 2:16-17.

143 See Ruth 1:1.

144 See Exodus 20:10 & Deuteronomy 5:14.

145 See Exodus 12:48-49 & Numbers 9:14.

146 See Deuteronomy 23:8-9.

147 See Deuteronomy 23:4.

148 See Deuteronomy 7:3-4 & 23:3-9.

149 Strong, James (1890), 'The Exhaustive Concordance of the Bible', Cincinnati: Jennings & Graham, reference 1484.

150 Strong, James (1890), 'The Exhaustive Concordance of the Bible', Cincinnati: Jennings & Graham - Strong's Concordance reference H1470 meaning 'a foreign nation; hence a Gentile' but also refers in the sense of massing i.e. a troop of animals or a flight of locusts.

second word is 'chananaios', which means a Canaanite or Phoenician[151]. The Gentiles then were all the other nations who did not worship the true God.

In the year 20-19 BC, King Herod began some significant renovations of the second Temple of Jerusalem. Everyone could enter the outer courtyard, which became known as the Courtyard of the Gentiles. It was an area that people could gather to ask questions about God to the rabbis of the Law. It was open to both Jews and Gentiles, circumcised and non-circumcised. There have been archaeological discoveries of 'warning stones' to warn non-Israelites about areas which they could not enter[152]. The scene of Jesus clearing out the Temple likely took place in this area on the day that He rode into Jerusalem on the donkey:

"And he was teaching them and saying to them, "Is it not written, 'My house shall be called a house of prayer for all the nations'? But you have made it a den of robbers"" Mark 11:17 ESV[153].

The word here used for 'peoples' is ethnos. A short time after this, Jesus is teaching about the parable of the vineyard. The owner sends one servant after another, and the workers beat them. He then sends his son whom they kill. After this, Jesus responded to the chief priests saying:

"Therefore I tell you, the kingdom of God will be taken away from you and given to a people[ethnos] producing its fruits" Matt 21:43 ESV.

The word for people yet again is ethnos, but this time in the singular form. Using it would have perhaps confused or angered those who heard him teach such a thing. Later, Peter wrote in his first epistle about how Jesus chose for himself a holy nation:

"'But you are a chosen race, a royal priesthood, a holy nation, a people for his own possession, that you may proclaim the excellencies of him who called you out of darkness into his marvelous light" 1 Peter 2:9 ESV

---

151 Strong, James (1890), 'The Exhaustive Concordance of the Bible', Cincinnati: Jennings & Graham, reference 5478

152 Zion, I. (2015) 'Ancient Temple Mount 'warning' stone is 'closest thing we have to the Temple', The Times of Israel. https://www.timesofisrael.com/ancient-temple-mount-warning-stone-is-closest-thing-we-have-to-the-temple/ 22 Oct 2015.

153 See also Isaiah 56:7.

In summary, all people groups who are not Jewish are called Gentiles. They are identified by where they come from but also their behaviour – in that they do not worship God. Even today, people recognise us by where we come from and how we behave – nation, ethnicity, race, religion. But our history is divided because of such divisions. One race persecutes another. One nation makes war against another. But Jesus announced a day where He would have a chosen people, a people who are not conformed or divided by the rules of any society. Indeed, I believe it is stated wonderfully in Galatians: *"There is neither Jew nor Gentile, neither slave nor free, nor is there male and female, for you are all one in Christ Jesus"* Gal 3:28 NIV.

"this small nation was one of the few places where the foul germs of anti-Semitism had found no fertile soil"

Rabbi Teddy Lewis

PHYSICAL BROTHERS: THE GENTILE BRIDES
CHAPTER 6

After defining in the last chapter Jews and Gentiles in relation in Israel, now I want to change the focus to similarities. Indeed, the central idea here in this section will be to discuss how Jew and Gentile are 'physical brothers'. I believe the best way to do this is by looking at Jesus, more specifically at His genealogy. While there are quite a few Gentile brides in the Bible such as Asenath and Zipporah, I want to focus on several brides that form part of the lineage of Jesus. There are two genealogies listed, one in the gospel of Matthew and the other in Luke. Some sceptics point at the differences between the two as a contradiction of the Bible. A straightforward solution to this, of course, is that one lists the lineage of Mary and other of Joseph.

These seven brides are not just historic people without meaning. Yes, each one is an ancestor of Jesus, but there is also a more profound meaning as events of their lives point to Jesus. I want to begin with **Eve**. She is the first mother of us all. She is both the mother of the Jewish race but also every human race, every human being. It began with God, who created Eve from Adam's rib:

"So the Lord God caused a deep sleep to fall upon the man, and while he slept took one of his ribs and closed up its place with flesh. And the rib that the Lord God had taken from the man he made into a woman and brought her to the man. Then the man said, "This at last is bone of my bones and flesh of my flesh; she shall be called Woman, because she was taken out of Man." Therefore a man shall leave his father and his

mother and hold fast to his wife, and they shall become one flesh" Genesis 2:21-24 ESV.

There are four events in Eve's life which allude to Jesus. After God takes Adam's rib to create Eve, his wound has to be closed up [his flesh was pierced]. Not only was Adam pierced, but also the second Adam. The bride of Jesus (the church) did not come to life until after He was pierced. Secondly, Adam is purposely put to sleep by God but then wakes and rises after to meet his bride. Perhaps, this too points to a spiritual change that occurred from Jesus' death to His resurrection.

Thirdly, God created Eve from the flesh of her husband. Likewise, Jesus taught *"Truly, truly, I say to you, unless you eat the flesh of the Son of Man and drink his blood, you have no life in you. Whoever feeds on my flesh and drinks my blood has eternal life, and I will raise him up on the last day. For my flesh is true food, and my blood is true drink. Whoever feeds on my flesh and drinks my blood abides in me, and I in him"* John 6:53-56 ESV.

The last allusion to Jesus occurs when sin comes into the world. Eve ate the fruit that was forbidden. Adam then ate the fruit, choosing to be in the same state as his bride. Possibly, he decided to take his course of action because he loved her so much. Perhaps, if Adam had not of eaten, God would have removed Eve from the garden and made a new wife for Adam from another rib. This view is symbolic of Jesus, as He chose to bear the sins of mankind out of love.

The second bride I want to discuss is **Rebecca**, the bride of Isaac. A central figure in this story is the servant of Abraham called Eliezer. Some have noted that we can view Eliezer as a representation of the Holy Spirit[154]. Eliezer means 'mighty, divine helper' a *type* of the Holy Spirit. I am not saying that Eliezer was the Holy Spirit, not at all. Instead, it is about saying that the record of him, on a deeper level, represents what the Holy Spirit does. Isaac is a type of Jesus. He went up on the hill as a sacrifice. God provided a Lamb. There is no mention in the text of Isaac's departure from the mountain. Instead, it says that Abraham came down with his servants. Isaac is not mentioned again until he is united with his bride. Jesus was our sacrificial Lamb, who ascended and will one day meet with His bride the church. This pattern of events is evident in the

---

154 Missler, Chuck. (2006) A Story of Bethlehem: The Kinsman-Redeemer, khouse [online] https://www.khouse.org/articles/2006/683/print/

Jewish tradition of betrothal and marriage. They have a betrothal/engagement, and then the groom goes to prepare a place, and when it is ready, he comes for her, and they have the wedding.

Abraham (the father) sent Eliezer (the helper/Holy Spirit) to choose a bride (church) for Isaac (Jesus). The servant chose Rebecca through an act of prayer. Believing Eliezer, she goes with him. Similarly, just before the ascension, Jesus prayed for his disciples saying: *"I have manifested your name to the people whom you gave me out of the world. Yours they were, and you gave them to me, and they have kept your word. Now they know that everything that you have given me is from you. For I have given them the words that you gave me, and they have received them and have come to know in truth that I came from you; and they have believed that you sent me"* John 17:6-8 ESV. Jesus chose his disciples, and they believed that the Father sent Him. The parallels are there.

Next, it is worthwhile noticing that Rebecca came out of Babylon. In the same way, the church [bride of Jesus] is coming out of a spiritual Babylon. The Babylon spirit is just as active in the earth today, if not even more so. Even the nations and state federations seem to still symbolize Babylon right through history, the Greek Empire, the Roman Empire, Nazi Germany and also the modern European Union. The call has always been there, *"Come out of her, my people, lest you take part in her sins, lest you share in her plagues"* Rev 18:4 ESV. Lastly, we should note that Isaac was returning from the well of living water, the well called Lahai-roi when he met Rebecca for the first time [Gen 24:65]. Jesus is dwelling at the well of living water. Indeed, He offers us living water and is preparing a place for us, for that day when He returns.

The third bride we should look at is **Rahab**. The Israelite's had crossed the river and went on to Gilgal to rededicate themselves. From there they would move on to face Jericho in battle, but first, they sent in spies. Rahab helped these spies to hide and then to escape from the city. Her house was part of the city wall. When an archaeological dig took place at Jericho, they found that the outer wall had collapsed except for a section where there were some houses. While the story may at first seem as simple as this, we must consider why God chose Rahab to be part of the lineage of Jesus. If we look a little closer, we find more allusions to the church.

We can note that Rahab was saved by faith, *"By faith Rahab the prostitute did not perish with those who were disobedient, because she had given a friendly welcome to the spies"* Hebrews 11:31 ESV. Yes, she had put faith in the men, but she also trusted in God. She declared *"I know that the Lord has given you the land, and that the fear of you has fallen upon us, and that all the inhabitants of the land melt away before you"* Joshua 2:9 ESV. She also added, *"soon as we heard it, our hearts melted, and there was no spirit left in any man because of you, for the Lord your God, he is God in the heavens above and on the earth beneath"* Joshua 2:11 ESV. So Rahab had heard and believed. Similarly, Hosea[155] talks poetically about a woman who becomes an adulterous woman and runs off with her lovers, before the Lord draws her back. Rahab was a prostitute who had now declared her faith in God and her life would never be the same, as she would become part of the people of the Lord. She was 'grafted in' because of her faith.

The fourth bride is **Ruth**. Her story resonates with the church perhaps more powerfully than all the other brides. Ruth, symbolizing the church, was brought in by Naomi who symbolizes Israel. Ruth was not brought in until Naomi was exiled. Ruth did not replace Naomi, but instead, she listened and learned. Likewise, the church continues a story that had begun with Adam, Abraham and Isaac. Naomi then remained an exile until Ruth was ready to become the bride of Boaz. Equivalently, we expect the Jews to embrace their Messiah as the church prepares to meet its groom. Ruth asked Boaz to put his garments over her [Ruth 3:8-9]. Then as well, we have been robed in Jesus' righteousness [Isaiah 61:10]. Boaz became Ruth's kinsman-redeemer. Jesus is our kinsman-redeemer who has paid the cost.

Next is **Bathsheba**, who became the bride of King David. Bathsheba, like Eve, is not directly mentioned in the lineage, but it was through her union with David that Solomon was born. Solomon and David both feature in Jesus' lineage. Bathsheba was a Gentile, the wife of Uriah the Hittite. David saw her bathing and desired her and took her, eventually arranging for the death of her husband. Many people have viewed the bath scene as seduction, but perhaps she was innocent. There are a couple of things to consider here. Firstly, the washing could be symbolic of baptism. Christians are baptised and will one day attend the marriage supper.

---

155 See Hosea 2.

The next thing to consider is that the Hebrew words for Beth and Bath are the same, and it means 'vessel' or 'house'. Sheba then means 'oath' and 'seven'. Join these together, and her name means 'house/vessel – the daughter of the oath'. Her name alludes to a significant well called Beersheba, the well of the oath, the well of seven, the well of fulfilment. David was the promised King to which people would compare all other Israeli Kings. Through his marriage to Bathsheba (the daughter of the oath), God would fulfil the promise and send the Messiah.

Tamar is the next bride, and her story is quite unusual as she conceived by her father-in-law, Judah:

"In the course of time the wife of Judah, Shua's daughter, died. When Judah was comforted, he went up to Timnah to his sheepshearers, he and his friend Hirah the Adullamite. And when Tamar was told, "Your father-in-law is going up to Timnah to shear his sheep," she took off her widow's garments and covered herself with a veil, wrapping herself up, and sat at the entrance to Enaim, which is on the road to Timnah. For she saw that Shelah was grown up, and she had not been given to him in marriage. When Judah saw her, he thought she was a prostitute, for she had covered her face. He turned to her at the roadside and said, "Come, let me come in to you," for he did not know that she was his daughter-in-law. She said, "What will you give me, that you may come in to me?" He answered, "I will send you a young goat from the flock." And she said, "If you give me a pledge, until you send it—" He said, "What pledge shall I give you?" She replied, "Your signet and your cord and your staff that is in your hand." So he gave them to her and went in to her, and she conceived by him. Then she arose and went away, and taking off her veil she put on the garments of her widowhood" Genesis 38:12-19 ESV.

But these peculiar events also reflect the church. Tamar had lost her husband and then her second husband. But she decided to lay aside her widowhood garment to abide with Judah. In the same manner, the church has also laid aside their old nature and is dressed in the new nature. It is an essential act in order to abide with her heavenly groom. They put on Jesus as their new garment *"But put on the Lord Jesus Christ"* Rom 13:14 ESV. Her second action of importance is that she covered her face with a veil. The church is also living in a mystery (or veil) till they meet with Jesus, the groom, face to face and see His full Glory and Majesty revealed. Paul wrote saying, *"And we all, with unveiled face, beholding the glory of the Lord, are being transformed into the same image from one degree of glory to another. For this comes from the Lord who is the Spirit"* 2 Corinthians 3:18 ESV. Lastly, Tamar sat down near the gates of Ainan on the way to Timnah. Ainan means 'two water wells', and this perhaps symbolizes the well of the Old Testament and the well of the New Testament.

In summary, we should consider both Jews and Gentiles as physical brothers. We all come from Adam, and we share a history together, and our hope is the same, the Messiah.

"The Irish journalist and playwright, Denis Johnston, was among the first to enter Buchenwald"[156] and witness the horrors of a concentration camp

156 *Keogh, D. (1998) 'Jews in Twentieth-Century Ireland', Cork University Press, pp193.*

SPIRITUAL BROTHERS: THE COVENANT
CHAPTER 7

One evening I went in to pray in the prayer room at our house and was bringing the days' events to the Lord in prayer. That day I had ordered some research books. I prayed and asked the Lord to continue to bring me to the right historical sources to do my research, but more importantly, to give me knowledge and revelation on the spiritual aspects. Then the Lord asked me to open my Bible and read Amos 1:9 (KJV), which says:

Thus said the LORD; For three transgressions of Tyrus, and for four, I will not turn away the punishment thereof; because they delivered up the whole captivity to Edom, and remembered not the brotherly covenant.

Immediately, the expression of the 'brotherly covenant' drew my attention. I had never noticed it before. Of this verse, Barnes[157] wrote *"It was not a covenant only, nor previous friendliness only; but a specific covenant, founded on friendship which they forgat and brake. If they retained the memory of Hiram's contact with David and Solomon, it was a sin against light too. After David had expelled the Jebusites from Jerusalem, "Hiram King of Tyre sent messengers to David, and cedar trees and carpenters and masons; and they built David a house"*[158]. The Philistines heard of the agreement and invaded but the Lord gave David

---

157 Barnes, A. (1834) Barnes Notes on the Old and New Testaments.

158 See 2 Samuel 5:11.

victory over them[159]. This recognition of him by Hiram was to David a proof, *"that the Lord had established him king over Israel, and that He had exalted his kingdom for His people, Israel's sake"*[160]. Here we see that Hiram had recognised David as King, and set about to establish a house for him. Not only that, but Hiram had also accepted God as God. We see this in a letter to David concerning Solomon "Because the Lord hath loved his people, He hath made thee king over them. Blessed be the Lord God of Israel, that made heaven and earth, who hath given to David a wise son - that he might build a house for the Lord" 2 Chron 2:11-12 KJV. Barnes[161] also noted that *"A later treaty, offered by Demetrius Nicator to Jonathan, makes detailed provision that the Jews should have "the feasts and sabbaths and new moons and the solemn days and the three days before the feast and the three days after the feast, as days of immunity and freedom."* So while we do not know the actual text of the 'brotherly covenant', there is a possibility that part of it allowed Jews who lived in Tyre to travel to Jerusalem for the religious festivals. However, the main focus of the agreement involved the supply of wood for the temple:

"You know that David my father could not build a house for the name of the Lord his God because of the warfare with which his enemies surrounded him, until the Lord put them under the soles of his feet. But now the Lord my God has given me rest on every side. There is neither adversary nor misfortune. And so, I intend to build a house for the name of the Lord my God, as the Lord said to David my father, 'Your son, whom I will set on your throne in your place, shall build the house for my name.' Now therefore command that cedars of Lebanon be cut for me. And my servants will join your servants, and I will pay you for your servants such wages as you set, for you know that there is no one among us who knows how to cut timber like the Sidonians." As soon as Hiram heard the words of Solomon, he rejoiced greatly and said, "Blessed be the Lord this day, who has given to David a wise son to be over this great people." And Hiram sent to Solomon, saying, "I have heard the message that you have sent to me. I am ready to do all you desire in the matter of cedar and cypress timber. My servants shall bring it down to the sea from Lebanon, and I will make it into rafts to go by sea to the place you direct. And I will have them broken up there, and you shall receive it. And you shall meet

---

159 See 2 Samuel 5.

160 See 2 Samuel 5:12.

161 Barnes, A. (1834) Barnes Notes on the Old and New Testaments.

my wishes by providing food for my household." So Hiram supplied Solomon with all the timber of cedar and cypress that he desired, while Solomon gave Hiram 20,000 cors of wheat as food for his household, and 20,000 cors of beaten oil. Solomon gave this to Hiram year by year. And the Lord gave Solomon wisdom, as he promised him. And there was peace between Hiram and Solomon, and the two of them made a covenant [treaty]." 1 Kings 5:3-12 ESV

Barnes[162] final comments on Amos 1:9 mention the punishment on Tyre for their breach of this agreement: *""This brotherly covenant Tyre remembered not," when they delivered up to Edom "a complete captivity," all the Jews who came into their hands. It seems then, that that covenant had a special provision against selling them away from their own land. This same provision other people made for love of their country or their homes; the Jews, for love of their religion. This covenant Tyre remembered not, but brake. They knew doubtless why Edom sought to possess the Israelites; but the covetousness of Tyre fed the cruelty of Edom, and God punished the broken appeal to Himself."*

I believe that they called it the 'brotherly covenant' because they perhaps saw each other as brothers. We see evidence of this when Hiram refers to Solomon as 'my brother'[163] and going by the words used by Hosea the 'brotherly' aspect had been mutual between them. You may wonder why two people might need to make such an agreement with each other. In our modern world, people make legal contracts with written documents. If any party breaches the agreement, then then the matter is settled in the courts. Yet going back in history, kingdoms did not make peaceful alliances in this way. Take Ireland, for example, where kings would often exchange relatives with other neighbouring kings to ensure peace. If the agreement was broken, they would kill the relatives. It was a simple but effective way of ensuring peace.

As for Hiram and Solomon, they made a covenant. Many people struggle with the concept of covenants, so let's look at them briefly before moving forward. A covenant usually consists of several elements, such as:

- It must be between two or more people.

---

162 Barnes, A. (1834) Barnes Notes on the Old and New Testaments.

163 אחי ' meaning 'my brother', see 1 Kings 9:13.

- The parties discuss and agree the terms.
- They conduct a ceremony to seal the covenant [blood sacrifice].
- There must be a physical sign.
- A covenant meal of confirmation.
- It involves a witness or witnesses.
- It spells out consequences for those who break it.
- There is a celebration meal.

Seeing how both Hiram and Solomon honoured God, I think it would be safe to assume that God was involved in their covenant. As previously mentioned, we do not know the terms of the agreement, but maybe we can make this conclusion because of what happened when Tyre broke the covenant. If the contract had not been made before God, then perhaps Tyre would not have received judgement for their actions. God takes covenant agreements seriously. In the time of Jeremiah, he petitioned king Zedekiah to set the slaves free. When the king agreed, he made a covenant agreement but then later broke it. God sent Jeremiah to declare judgment upon the king for his breach of the covenant:

"*Therefore, thus says the Lord: You have not obeyed me by proclaiming liberty, every one to his brother and to his neighbour; behold, I proclaim to you liberty to the sword, to pestilence, and to famine, declares the Lord. I will make you a horror to all the kingdoms of the earth. And the men who transgressed my covenant and <u>did not keep the terms of the covenant</u> that they made before me, I will make them like the calf that they cut in two and passed between its parts— the officials of Judah, the officials of Jerusalem, the eunuchs, the priests, and all the people of the land who passed between the parts of the calf. And I will give them into the hand of their enemies and into the hand of those who seek their lives. Their dead bodies shall be food for the birds of the air and the beasts of the earth. And Zedekiah king of Judah and his officials I will give into the hand of their enemies and into the hand of those who seek their lives, into the hand of the army of the king of Babylon which has withdrawn from you. Behold, I will command, declares the Lord, and will bring them back to this city. And they will fight against it and take it and burn it with fire. I will make the cities of Judah a desolation without inhabitant"* Jeremiah 34:17-22 ESV.

Apart from the judgement of the people, the city, or indeed the land would face fire and the strongholds, would be torn down. Does this differ at all from what happened to Tyre for their breach of the brotherly covenant: *"I will send a fire upon the wall of Tyre, and it shall devour her strongholds"* Amos 1:9-10 ESV.

It is important to note that during the three-year ministry of Jesus, He visited Tyre and Sidon. An immediate thought might be, that He went there to minister to the Jews that lived there. However, we see from the gospels (Matthew 15:21; Mark 7:24) that Jesus healed a Gentile. Indeed, many people in the area came forth to hear him preach (Mark 3:8; Gospel of Luke 6:17, Matthew 11:21–23). Perhaps this was one example that the disciples thought of when they later considered if the Gospel was for the Gentiles. Many times, Jesus displayed His love for both Jew and Gentile. However, with Tyre, I think perhaps that something deeper is going on that we must explore.

Therefore, I believe that we should look a bit deeper into the history of Tyre but perhaps also examine what Tyre might symbolise itself. Tyre was a small plot of land located on the border of Asher. It was independent of Israel and part of the Phoenician Empire. The people of Sidon colonised the city, and they named the city of Sidon after the great-grandson of Noah [Genesis 10:15-19]. After the Israelites entered the Promised Land, the tribe of Asher was unable to drive them out [Judges 1:31-32], which is why Isaiah referred to Tyre as the 'virgin daughter of Sidon' [Isaiah 23:12]. So, the Phoenicians must have had a mighty empire and strongly fortified cities. Indeed, the word 'Tyre' means rock, which comes from the offshore rocky formation where the people constructed the town. Alexander the Great built a causeway during his siege of the city[164] to ensure a win. The land bridge joined together the offshore settlement with a coastal city which had also sprung up, called Ushu. City merchants began to venture out around the Mediterranean and established colonies on islands and even on the coasts of Northern Africa and Spain[165].

One significant impact that the Phoenicians empire had upon the modern world stems from its language. The Phoenicians used a twenty-

---

164 Presutta, David (2007) 'The Biblical Cosmos Versus Modern Cosmology', page 225, referencing: Katzenstein, H.J., (1973) 'The History of Tyre', p.9.

165 Easton, M G (1897) 'Tyre', Easton's Bible Dictionary.

two-letter alphabet [no vowels], and it was very similar to the Hebrew language. To an untrained person like myself, the two alphabets are almost the same, except that one looks tidier than the other. However, some scholars such as Solomon Birnbaum would make a case that the two alphabets are completely different[166]. The Phoenician language thrived in the 9th century BC and became part of other languages, including Greek. Greek was the Beginning of most European languages, including Latin, Celtic, Slavic, Turkic, Armenian, Baltic, Cyrillic.

At the centre of the religion of Tyre was the 'Lord of Tyre', a god called Melqart. The Greeks and Romans perhaps saw this god as being a Tyrian type of 'Hercules'. Indeed, when the historian Herodotus travelled to Tyre, it was because of interest in a temple there dedicated to Hercules. Instead, he discovered that their Hercules was much older and somewhat different from the Greek Hercules[167]. Some have said that Elijah's comments about Baal's journeys suggest that the Baal in question was Melqart. Just after Elijah's stay with a widow in the Phoenician city Zarephath [Sarepta] he went down to challenge Ahab, and he mocked the prophets of Baal saying: *"Cry aloud, for he is a god. Either he is musing, or he is relieving himself, or he is on a journey, or perhaps he is asleep and must be awakened"* 1 Kings 18:27 ESV. If Elijah had previously been unaware of Tyrian pagan gods, then he would have learnt about them while staying with the widow. We must also remember that Ahab's wife, Jezebel, was daughter to the king of Tyre[168]. It was Jezebel that cast her influence upon him to mix the worship of Yahweh with the worship of Baal. With these points in mind, one could certainly believe that Melqart was the Baal of the Bible.

It was at this point that this history began to grab me because our previous journey 'turas' led us to stand against the spiritual powers of witchcraft in Europe. While on that journey, one central Biblical character was Elijah when he made a stand against those same powers in his day. Now they are coming up again as part of this new journey, not as something new, but more of a continuation of the information that the Lord had led us to previously. Even more significant than the link here to Elijah from our last journey was the legend of Europa. One night I was

---

166 The Hebrew scripts, Volume 2, Salomo A. Birnbaum, Palaeographia, 1954, "To apply the term Phoenician to the script of the Hebrews is hardly suitable. I have therefore coined the term Palaeo-Hebrew."

167 Euterpe, by Herodotus [2.44].

168 See 1Kings 16:31.

praying and was talking to the Lord about the research for this book, and I asked him not just for knowledge but for revelation, and God immediately led me to another piece of information about Tyre. Tyre was the birthplace of Europa! "The Myth tells the story of a young maiden called Europa, who captures the attention of Jupiter (or Zeus). He disguises himself as a bull (white/red) and convinces her to come with her. She rides his back, but when he has her trapped on an island, he rapes her[169]". People like Herodotus thought that the myth was just part of a tit for tat story of women stealing between Crete and Tyre[170]. However, as I found before from my previous journey, the myth somehow speaks towards the spiritual powers at work in Europe.

It was my conclusion concerning Europe, as it is of many others that it is the mystery Babylon. However, I do not believe that this is restricted to Europe alone but that it can also be applied elsewhere. Now that we have a link of Europa to Tyre, it makes our previous findings more significant because Revelation chapter 18 alludes extensively to the mercantile description of Tyre in Ezekiel chapters 26-28. The challenge we face today of defying our modern spiritual Babylon is not a main topic for this book as I wrote extensively about it in 'A Journey to Defy Witchcraft'. It is worthwhile mentioning it to see how this new journey connects to our last one, and indeed to the one before. God is good, and He leads us on a lifetime journey of discovery.

Returning to the idea of the brotherly covenant, this is how I am envisaging it spiritually. There is a brotherly bond between Israel (representing the Jews) and Tyre (embodying the Gentiles and Europe – through which most of the modern church springs from). The 'brothers' were initially supposed to work together for God, but they have instead broken their brotherly bonds and aimed to tear down and destroy each other. Throughout the centuries, both sides have committed horrific crimes. But God has not forsaken either the Gentiles or the Jews. As we draw closer towards the Lord's return, perhaps now is time for the two brothers to reconcile with each other. Indeed, it is time for them both to open a door of repentance and forgiveness to each other.

Isaiah spoke saying, "And the foreigners who join themselves to the LORD, to minister to him, to love the name of the LORD, and to be His

---

169 Harper, M. (2018) 'A Journey to Defy Witchcraft', Revival Well, pp. ix.

170 Davies, N. (2014) 'The Legend of Europa', Europe: A History, Boxley Head (ppXVI).

servants, everyone who keeps the Sabbath and does not profane it, and holds fast my covenant— these I will bring to my holy mountain, and make them joyful in my house of prayer; their burnt offerings and their sacrifices will be accepted on my altar; for my house shall be called a **house of prayer for all peoples**" Isaiah 56:6-7 ESV. The history of the Jews and Gentiles shows hostility against one another when sojourning in each other's lands. At first, they treat each other with suspicion and contempt, followed by harsh words and threats, and then with violence and persecution. But we are no longer foreigners to each other anymore. The writer of Hebrews spoke of Noah and Abraham and how they *"acknowledged that they were strangers and exiles on the earth"* Hebrews 11:13 ESV. Therefore let us have our identity first in Christ our Messiah, cultural and racial considerations must be secondary. All of us are in the same boat which is travelling through this world. For our hearts must desire a *"better country, that is, a heavenly one"* Hebrews 11:16 ESV. Let's no longer try and keep people out of the boat by exclusion or denial, but gather in as many souls as we travel by.

"Between 1933 and 1939, an estimated 439,000 Jews were forced to emigrate from countries in Europe with strong anti-Semitic laws"[171]

171 Keogh, D. (1998) 'Jews in Twentieth-Century Ireland', Cork University Press,pp142.

BROTHERS: BEHAVIOUR PATTERNS
CHAPTER 8

I grew up with two brothers. Looking back, one might notice patterns of behaviour between siblings. There are some prevailing theories about siblings in society. One theory I heard was that the 'firstborn' looks like the father more than the children to follow. Then comes the second child, the prevailing theory about the second child is the 'middle child syndrome', which of course could be applied to my life as I was the middle brother. Then you have the 'baby' of the family, and the theory is they get away with everything. The 'middle child syndrome' is apparently created by how parents treat the other two. The firstborn is prone to receiving privileges and responsibility. Meanwhile, the youngest child often receives indulgences.

To some extent, these stereotypes do speak somewhat into my childhood, but having become a parent, you get to understand the other side of the coin. The first child comes along, and you have a baby shower, you take a million photos, all their stuff is brand new. The second child arrives, there's no baby shower, you're so busy juggling a toddler and a newborn, you don't take as many photos. Most of what you give the new addition are hand-me-downs as there are no point re-buying things you kept safe for reuse, and other clothes from extended family might also come your way. With two children, one can less afford to buy everything new. The third baby perhaps comes a few years later, a broader gap in age difference. By the time they reach secondary school, the other two who went ahead might be finished school, or perhaps have even moved out or gone to college. Their departures can free up money and resources which the 'baby' will gladly take. The parents won't hold it back, because if they had that money when the other two were at that stage, they would have treated them too.

You may have identified some of these patterns as being relevant to your own experiences, either as you grew up, or when you became a parent. It's not my plan in this chapter to focus on natural siblings, but rather on behavioural patterns which may have been evident between Jews and Gentiles. But I do feel that these behaviours may somewhat resemble the kind of interactions that you may witness in the average family: play scenarios or disagreements, accidents, good times, bad times, or even tragedies.

Slavery

Growing up, you may never have gone to the extreme of calling your brother a slave. You may, however, have played a game called 'follow the leader'. You may also have made bargains, such as selling something you own to a sibling in exchange for their service (e.g. making beds or pocket money). You may have used your physical strength to overpower a sibling to force them to do something – such as to hand over a remote control for the TV. These kinds of interactions would happen daily, varying in severity and mostly harmless. There are, of course, instances where something more serious happens.

In the Bible, we have an example of slavery amongst siblings by looking at the life of Joseph and his brothers. Joseph was favoured by his father and hence became the focus of his brothers' anger. He received an expensive coat. Joseph also explained his dreams to his family, but they responded negatively. Eventually, his brothers threw him down into a pit and discussed killing him. Instead, they sold him as a slave. In Egypt, he faced several hardships, but thanks to God's help, Joseph prospered and helped the Egyptians. Through his role as second in command, other nations were blessed. What then should he do with his brothers when they come to buy food? If he had of acted in the flesh, Joseph could have put them all to death. Instead, he saw the wider picture and what God had planned through the difficult circumstances.

We can apply this logic to the relationship between Jews and Gentiles. Previously we identified 'sojourners' as being Gentiles who are either travelling through Israel or are living there as residents. God had given specific commands to the Israelites about their treatment. The book of Exodus records that they are commanded not to "oppress" a sojourner[172]. The Israelites should be accommodating and "know the heart of a sojourner" because they were also once sojourners in Egypt. In certain circumstances, Israelites were permitted to have sojourners as hired servants or as slaves. For example, the Hittites ended up as slaves instead of being destroyed[173]. Slavery in this era was not like the slavery of our modern times. The people were obliged to treat their slaves well and to release them after their servitude was complete, such as in the year of jubilee[174]. Over time, social barriers became muddled through marriages, such as King David and Bathsheba.

I find it interesting that God tells Israel that if they do not follow His Commandments that there will be judgments against them. One of the 'curses' mentioned is that *"the sojourner who is among you shall rise higher and higher above you, and you shall come down lower and lower"* Deuteronomy 28:43 ESV. Imagine telling your child that their punishment was that their sibling was now going to be their boss. If you look through history, it might be possible to highlight different events between communities, nations, or races that display such a shift.

Foreigners were not allowed to be the king of Israel[175] but if you think about it, human kings were never the ideal choice at all, whether Jew or Gentile. But because the Israelites demanded it, God allowed it, but they were told that their king must be "whom the Lord your God will choose". We can apply this to our own lives. It is now a common belief that our lives are our own and you can do what you want with it. Quite often, people choose for themselves a king too – a role model, sports team, or celebrity, or religious figure – who they allow to guide and shape their life choices. But our calling is to submit to will of the perfect King - Jesus.

---

172 See Exodus 22:21,23:9 & Deuteronomy 24:14.

173 See 1 Kings 9:20-21.

174 See Leviticus 25:40.

175 See Deuteronomy 17:5.

Harm

Sadly, there are times where siblings may end up injuring one another. It might be just minor physical injury or something more serious. There are also other types of injuries, such as emotional and psychological scars, often carried from childhood into adulthood. I can remember several occasions from my childhood where 'play' got out of hand, and one of us ended up hurt. Later in teen years, social behaviour can drive wedges between siblings, but we should not leave familial relationships in a state of disrepair. As believers, it is imperative for us to forgive and to love one another. When anger manifests as harm, the situation has gone beyond oppression or 'slavery'.

Once again, we have a Biblical example, that of Cain and Abel. It is the first instance of sibling rivalry, and it is also the first record we have of a murder. Cain and Abel both came to make sacrifices to the Lord. Cain worked with crops, but Abel was a herder/shepherd who tended flocks. Abel's sacrifice was deemed acceptable to the Lord, but He rejected Cain's. Was it rejected because of what it was, or because of the heart of the one offering it? I would say it was the latter. Instead of the brother dealing with the issues of his heart humbly before God, he decided to take it out on the one who was right with God. Anger is often a symptom of a deeper issue, whether that be unforgiveness or jealousy. Often people blame others, but the problem is that they are not right with God. The person that the anger is aimed at is immaterial really. If that person didn't exist, they would point the finger elsewhere. Cain killed Abel and he suffered consequences for the rest of his life. But God also showed him mercy, allowing no one to kill him.

In the Book of Deuteronomy, the judges were charged to *"Hear the cases between your brothers, and judge righteously between a man and his brother or the alien who is with him"* Deuteronomy 1:16 ESV. Cases were to be heard fairly, whether that involved Israelites or Gentiles. Gentiles were entitled to use the cities of refuge if they accidentally killed someone[176]. If a father is resolving an issue between two sons, is it not fair to listen to both sides, examine the evidence and then decide? The only perfect justice is God's justice. Humanity has attempted to

---

176 See Numbers 35:15.

reproduce justice, but it so very often fails. If everyone loved God and loved their neighbours, the world would be such a different place and brothers would be at peace with one another. God has provided us with clear instructions, that *"When a stranger sojourns with you in your land, you shall not do him wrong"* Leviticus 19:33 ESV. If the Gentiles sojourn in Israel, then they should be treated fairly. If a Jew should sojourn in a Gentile nation, they too should be treated fairly and not harmed. The rule applies to everyone.

Greed

Another commonplace occurrence between siblings is arguing over belongings. The property could be a toy, a piece of clothing, the last chicken wing on the serving plate, over bedrooms, and even over inheritance. One declares 'this is mine and not yours' and a struggle begins, often with one injured party who feels like they have been unfairly treated. Land debates are central to our modern political debates, especially concerning Israel. But land debates between Jew and Gentile go way back in history. God gave the 'Promised Land' to Israel, but Gentiles had previously owned it. Later, because Israel failed to obey God, Gentiles took the land. This land dispute also occurs in European history. One buys or takes land, and the other seizes it back.

The Biblical example I would like to use here is the parable of the Prodigal son. There are two sons, brothers, and both have a rich inheritance. One decides to take his inheritance and go off to have an easy life, only to lose it all. The other brother works hard and serves the father diligently. The son returns, and the father welcomes him home, but the brother scorns him because he feels as though his brother should have nothing. The father reminds him then that everything he owns is his, but it is right to celebrate the return of one who was lost.

Siblings caught up in debates of property ownership can easily reach the point where there is a complete breakdown in their relationship. But family should matter more than wealth. When Abraham came to the land of Canaan, he bought a field saying, *"I am a sojourner and foreigner among you; give me property among you for a burying place, that I may bury my dead out of my sight"* Genesis 23:4 ESV. Why did he buy a piece of land when God had given him that whole land as his inheritance[177] ? Abraham was a sojourner, and he knew his descendants would also be sojourners in Egypt[178]. The main thing here is that Israel does not belong to anyone. It belongs to God. The Israelites are told *"The land shall not be sold in perpetuity, for the land is mine. For you are strangers and sojourners with me"* Leviticus 25:23 ESV. I believe that Abraham understood that he would always be a sojourner with God, and while knowing that his descendants would be sojourners, he probably hoped that they too would walk with God. The Gentile inclusion[179] is not so that the Gentile people can own Israel. Rather our inclusion is so that we can sojourn with the Lord. Israel is the Lord's and squabbling over it in this sense is pointless.

Holiness

There is often a dispute between siblings regarding their behaviour. The standard of behaviour is set by parents, but often the expectation is perceived differently by each child. If they children have been misbehaving, the eldest one may get all the blame for something the younger ones did. They might say 'You are the eldest, and you should have known better'. In other cases, the eldest might start laying down the law for the others and demanding obedience 'or I'll tell daddy'. One child might perceive that they are called to be righteous [following the rules], and because of it think they are better than the others.

In the history of Jews and Gentiles, perhaps there is an expectation from the Jewish side that 'I am holy but not you'. Outsiders including sojourners were not allowed to *"draw near to burn incense before the LORD, lest he become like Korah and his company"* Numbers 16:40 ESV. In some instances, such as setting up and taking down the tabernacle, if outsiders came near, they were to be put to death[180]. Perhaps outsiders were kept at a distance because they had a real lack of

---

177 See Genesis 12:1.

178 See Genesis 15:13.

179 Sojourners in Israel were given the option to be circumcised and be "as a native of the land", see Exodus 12:48-51.

180 See Numbers 1:51.

understanding of the faith of Israel. But I would suggest that it was not exclusionary – in that the Gentiles were kept away in all circumstances.

Let's have a further look, God had instructed the Israelites, *"You shall not eat anything that has died naturally. You may give it to the sojourner who is within your towns, that he may eat it, or you may sell it to a foreigner. For you are a people holy to the LORD your God"* Deuteronomy 14:21 ESV. One might read this and feel that it implies that the Israelites were called to be holy, but not the Gentiles. But that is not quite the application at all. God clearly gave other commandments which included outsiders, *"But you shall keep my statutes and my rules and do none of these abominations, either the native or the stranger who sojourns among you"* Leviticus 18:26 ESV. Sojourners could adhere to a cleansing process[181] and observe the sabbath[182] and could make a food offering[183]. So, were the Gentiles to keep the rules or not? There were ones who turned to God and were circumcised. But others, who had no interest in God, or the religious practices of Israel were given the meat that everyone else would not eat.

"There shall be one law for the native and for the stranger who sojourns among you[184]*"* Exodus 12:49 ESV.

So, what happened to Gentiles who had chosen not to assimilate to the faith of the Israelites, and then committed sin in the land. If they did not know that it was a sin, then this was 'unintentional sin' which was covered by a sacrifice to the Lord made by the community as a whole [185]. But the sojourners were treated differently, which would have caused social issues. In modern day Israel, the Ethiopian Jews who were rescued in 1991 have been left in a state of social decay with little empathy from the wider public. Education, unemployment, and imprisonment are the biggest challenges facing them. When I was in Israel, I met a pastor whose ministry was to Ethiopian youths to try and help them reach for a brighter future.

I think that we need to let it sink in that the ministry of Jesus was both to Jew and Gentile. Jesus did not adhere to social divides

---

181 See Leviticus 17:15.

182 Leviticus 16:29, Exodus 20:10

183 Numbers 15:14, Leviticus 17:8-9

184 See Leviticus 17:10-12 as an example of rules applicable to anyone who was in the land.

185 See Numbers 15:22-31.

surrounding ethnicity, gender, or race. These interactions would have been shocking to his disciples and others who witnessed them. He helped a Roman centurion[186] by healing his servant. Jesus spoke to a Samaritan woman at a well. His miracle of the loaves and the fishes took place on the eastern side of the Sea of Galilee, which was in Gentile territory. He helped the daughter of a Gentile woman[187] and then visited the Gentile city Sidon[188].

It was not until years later when Peter had revelation from God[189] about the Gentiles accepting the word of God. Paul challenged the leaders at a council in Jerusalem, Peter said, *"he did not discriminate between us and them, for he purified their hearts by faith"* Acts 15:9 NIV. James added, *"It is my judgment, therefore, that we should not make it difficult for the Gentiles who are turning to God. Instead we should write to them, telling them to abstain from food polluted by idols, from sexual immorality, from the meat of strangled animals and from blood"* Acts 15:19-20 NIV. In the same way that James realised that they should not make it difficult for the Gentiles to turn to God, neither should we make it difficult for the Jews to do likewise.

Apart, then together

Perhaps the journey of Jew and Gentile is prophetically displayed by the lives of Jacob and Esau. The twins were noted for fighting in the womb and the fighting continued after their birth. Jacob tricked his brother out of his birth right and inheritance and fled for fear of his brother's retribution. The two went their separate ways and were apart for many years. But the Lord led them back to reconciliation, just as He is now leading Jews and Gentiles to reconcile. The first part of that reconciliation was a desire in the hearts of both men to be at peace with one another. Jacob sent a message ahead of him saying that he wanted to find favour with Esau[190]. When Jacob heard that his brother was

---

186 See Matthew 8:5-13.

187 See Mark 7:25-30.

188 See Mark 7:31.

189 See Acts 11.

190 See Exodus 32:5.

coming to meet him, he was in great "fear and distress". When we step out to reconcile with someone, there is a moment, perhaps when we sit waiting for them to arrive when bad memories, doubt, fear can flood our minds. The second step that Jacob took was generosity. Jacob sent ahead of himself livestock and gifts for his brother[191].

In the Old Testament, God gave instructions regarding generosity, such as:

- Not stripping vineyard bare but allowing a portion for the poor and the sojourner[192].
- If your brother becomes poor, to support him like a sojourner, to feed him and allow him to live with you[193].
- To give part of the tithe to sojourners, orphans, and widows[194].
- To not gather a full harvest, whether sheaves, olives or grapes but allow the sojourners, orphans, and widows to have some[195].
- To not reap the field right to the edge but to leave gleanings for the poor and the sojourner[196].

But there was still no guarantee that it would go well. Why did he choose generosity above other ways of tackling disputes? Perhaps he felt like he had stolen from his brother and was returning to him what was due in the hope of peace. I believe that generosity can be an

---

191 See Exodus 32:13-16.

192 And you shall not strip your vineyard bare, neither shall you gather the fallen grapes of your vineyard. You shall leave them for the poor and for the sojourner: I am the Lord your God. Leviticus 19:10 ESV

193 "If your brother becomes poor and cannot maintain himself with you, you shall support him as though he were a stranger and a sojourner, and he shall live with you. Leviticus 25:35 ESV

194 "When you have finished paying all the tithe of your produce in the third year, which is the year of tithing, giving it to the Levite, the sojourner, the fatherless, and the widow, so that they may eat within your towns and be filled, Deuteronomy 26:12 ESV

195 "When you reap your harvest in your field and forget a sheaf in the field, you shall not go back to get it. It shall be for the sojourner, the fatherless, and the widow, that the Lord your God may bless you in all the work of your hands. When you beat your olive trees, you shall not go over them again. It shall be for the sojourner, the fatherless, and the widow. When you gather the grapes of your vineyard, you shall not strip it afterward. It shall be for the sojourner, the fatherless, and the widow. Deuteronomy 24:19-21 ESV

196 "And when you reap the harvest of your land, you shall not reap your field right up to its edge, nor shall you gather the gleanings after your harvest. You shall leave them for the poor and for the sojourner: I am the Lord your God." Leviticus 23:22 ESV

expression of love. Jesus talked about this saying, *"For I was hungry and you gave me food, I was thirsty and you gave me drink, I was a stranger and you welcomed me"* Matthew 25:35 ESV. What Jacob needed was a greater understanding of God.

Then that night, Jacob met with God and wrestled with him. Jacob was blessed and given a new name, Israel. Jacob had been wrestling with the power of his flesh throughout his life. It was with cunning that he had outdone his brother. He aimed to achieve the birth right through his own strength and had not trusted in God to give it to him.

Jacob's inheritance, and ours, was not the value of the land of Israel, but it was to know God. We are not called to focus on ownership of materials in this life (beyond our needs) but we should concentrate on heavenly things. The author of Philippians wrote that *"our citizenship is in heaven, and from it we await a Saviour, the Lord Jesus Christ"* Philippians 3:20 ESV[197]. Kind David wrote, *"I am a sojourner on the earth; hide not your commandments from me"* Psalm 119:19 ESV. Now we can walk closely with God and know him. Paul wrote *"But now in Christ Jesus you who once were far off have been brought near by the blood of Christ"* Ephesians 2:13 ESV.

Because Jesus looked past the social divides, there will be people in heaven from every nation, race and tongue. How can we ignore how God sees us all? Yes, we do naturally get drawn to index people into categories. It is how our brains work. If we didn't categorize everything our brains would overload. But categorizing simplifies truth and this is where prejudice begins, and when mixed with hatred, its where racism starts. Often when I meet with new people in church circles, one of the first questions I hear is "what church do you go to?" Whatever I answer, the question aims to place me into a category and assign a pre-set list of attributes. This simplification often ends up with wrong assumptions made about others, not just in churches, but in society.

---

197 See also Ephesians 2:19 ESV, "So then you are no longer strangers and aliens, but you are fellow citizens with the saints and members of the household of God."

"Beloved, I urge you as sojourners and exiles
to abstain from the passions of the flesh,
which wage war against your soul" 1 Peter 2:11 ESV.

"Hear my prayer, O LORD,
and give ear to my cry;
hold not your peace at my tears!
For I am a sojourner with you,
a guest, like all my fathers" Psalm 39:12 ESV.

"There is neither Jew nor Greek,
there is neither slave nor free,
there is no male and female,
for you are all one in Christ Jesus" Galatians 3:28 ESV.

Lord, help us to change,
So that we look beyond social divides,
And walk-through life as a sojourner with You.

FOURTEEN CITIES
CHAPTER 9

In 2019, I began to feel called to go to the city walls. At first, I did not know why, but the understanding came later. So, I had to just act in obedience, to go to the right places at the right time. The first issue is that there are not fourteen cities in Ireland in our modern definition of a city. I prayed about it and came out with a list. Some are physical cities, but others are towns which have Cathedrals and a sense of authority over an area of population. Seven of these were in Northern Ireland and seven in the South. I would have liked to have made a list of all these places, and then come up with a plan. That was not how the Lord wanted me to operate. Instead, it was usually the week of the visit that I felt it on my heart to go to a particular place, and I just obeyed and went. It seemed that it had to happen in a specific order as directed by the Lord.

I had already travelled to several of these cities before the Lord informed me of the purpose. I was on a journey akin to Nehemiah. After the Israelites had spent many years in captivity and oppression, Nehemiah became burdened for his nation after hearing awful news from fellow countrymen who had travelled there. Overcome with sadness, he sought the face of the Lord and wept. Then the king noticed that Nehemiah was downcast, which led to permission to return to his land to rebuild the wall and the Temple. When he travelled to Jerusalem, he first went around the city to examine the walls before talking with the community who would eventually do the repairs[198]. Then he declares to them *"You see the trouble we are in, how Jerusalem lies in ruins with its gates burned. Come, let us build the wall of Jerusalem, that we may no longer suffer derision"* Nehemiah 2:17 ESV. Then he shared the vision with them and how God had opened the door with the king for provision. First came a heart for his nation, then intercession and weeping with God for his land, then a journey to see the state of his city, followed by a sharing of his vision and how God was going to change things. Now, this journey had become my journey.

By September, I had visited the last city. Then during prayer, the Lord told me that if I check back through my journal from December the previous year, I will see an alignment to what he was saying to me then with what he showed me about each city. I was very excited and somewhat overcome by the idea. Back in December 2018, I had taken fourteen days to pray. The Lord wanted me to review that time with Him. When I got home from work that day, I went digging for my journal. The Lord had spoken to me so much during those fourteen days that I had filled a whole journal and I knew that at some point I would return to review and share with others what He had said to me.

I opened my notes from my first day of prayer. God had shown me that in my childhood I had a heart for him even when I was young. I had a good foundation but had been enticed to a life of sin. That was also what the Lord had shown me at the first city, Drogheda. I was astonished and thanked God. Then He told me to check something else. Several times He had spoken to me through visions about being a watchman on the wall. When I checked back through three different journals, I found that it had also been fourteen times. Shockingly, these fourteen lined up also. I was amazed. It's like layers.

God had connected this journey of mine with the missions of other intercessors in 2019. On top of this, God had put down layers of information, visions, verses, prayers in my daily walk with Him and I had

198 See also Nehemiah 2:13-16 (ESV): "I went out by night by the Valley Gate to the Dragon Spring and to the Dung Gate, and I inspected the walls of Jerusalem that were broken down and its gates that had been destroyed by fire. Then I went on to the Fountain Gate and to the King's Pool, but there was no room for the animal that was under me to pass. Then I went up in the night by the valley and inspected the wall, and I turned back and entered by the Valley Gate, and so returned. And the officials did not know where I had gone or what I was doing, and I had not yet told the Jews, the priests, the nobles, the officials, and the rest who were to do the work."

not noticed. God is amazing. These interconnects & layers created a re-alignment.

But these multiple layers posed a challenge, how could I express the information? After much prayer on the matter, I decided to do it in a poetic form, with details provided in the references. The cities will be in the same order as my visits. Then after each trip, I will share about my day of prayer and about being a watchman.

O ancient stronghold of **Drogheda**[199],
Where the enemy encamped against my people
And threw us down.
It was because of our sins that Cromwell came[200],
But he did more than justice
And established injustice.
He came to the corner of the city,
Not because it was weak,
But because it was strong,
It was the place where the church stood.
The watchman would have stood on that wall and shouted,
'Cromwell has come, Cromwell is here!'
Men would have rushed to the defences,
But Cromwell's cannons broke the church and the walls,
A repeated story across the land.

---

199 Visited Drogheda on the 27th March 2019.

200 Stated by synod of Irish churches prior to his arrival.

But now Lord, Your watchman returns,
Not in a time of war,
For I hear the birds singing their praise to You.
But beyond this wall is another generation
Whose morals have been falling,
Yes, to get drunk and take drugs and fornicate.
A stronghold of the church has turned to a hotbed of sin.
Look and see the new church built,
For its windows are barred,
But there is an open gate
To those who seek to remember
And know the past.
I seek that knowledge.
"Behold my city,
The one whom I lifted up,
And established
By the throes of a mighty river.
But you worshipped the god
Of that river,
And hoped not in Me,
But in the strength of your own hands.
Therefore, you saw
Your stronghold
Torn down.
You said, 'Look I am
Within my fortification,
What can do me harm?'[201]
But it was made low.
Now my watchman return,
For so shall an enemy return,
They shall contend for the strongholds of this land[202].

---

201 The people were misled when they were told "the Lord will deliver us" [see Isa 36:18].

202 Isa 36:1 ESV "In the fourteenth year of King Hezekiah, Sennacherib king of Assyria came up against all the fortified cities of Judah and took them".

You shall cry out 'lookout' and 'beware',
And this generation shall hear their cry
carried on the wind."

The Lord then instructed me to go and stand in the ruins of the old church, and so I did.

"The wall is old and unsupported,
broken and falling apart.
But look and see this supporting wall,
It supports the old wall,
So that it does not crumble.
So, go and stand by the wall of my
Stronghold in Ireland
To rebuild, repair and support.
Now look out the window and see where the city wall stood."

I declared 'My Lord will rebuild His Fortress,
His stronghold in this city.
The foundation stone is good!'

Ireland is like a man lying in the water
Floating in the flow of a river[203].
It is time to jump in the river,
Time to hear and see,
With a new perspective.
You will hear the sound of the blowing wind!
You will hear the sound of creaking and groaning
And float upon His supportive flow,
No longer leaning on your own feet.
Let's go, my Lord, let's go!
Then I heard the Lord say:

"It's time to review
The things that I have said to you,
And the things that I have shown you.

203 A vision during a time of prayer on the 14th Dec 2018.

And I will restore you,
I will sanctify you,
I will come to you."
So, I asked the Lord, 'What shall we review?'
He responded **"Everything.**
I will speak to you and reveal a deeper
Meaning of the things I have shown you,
A deeper place."
I prayed, 'Let Your Will be done, where will we start[204]?'
Then I saw my land and my people,
As if they were a little boy sat on the stairs
Sitting within earshot of a prayer meeting.
In their youth, they had a desire to know and love God,
But they have been overcome by evil and deceived.
Then I saw my land and my people,
As if a boy stood alone in a forest,
Unafraid of the darkness,
And with a desire to seek God
Outside of traditions.
Then I saw my land and my people
As if a young boy at school
Playing joyfully with the other nations as a leader.
Evidently from a young age,
My people and my nation have had a desire for God.
But the calling has been interrupted
by many bad choices.
Oh Lord set us upon Your Precepts[205],
Upon Your Laws,
Upon Your example,
Lead me, Lord, I pray.

---

204 Proverbs 3:5-6 ESV "Trust in the Lord with all your heart, and do not lean on your own understanding. In all your ways acknowledge him, and he will make straight your paths."

205 Proverbs 4:18 ESV "But the path of the righteous is like the light of dawn, which shines brighter and brighter until full day."

No one within Your grasp will You ever let fall.
They are secure, and they are safe, chosen and saved.
If You hold the boat in Your Hand,
Even if the world should move, will the boat sink?
Ireland was never in trouble
Or in danger.
It was just being shaped,
Refined, made ready,
Prepared.

*"**prayers** also shall be made for him continually;*
and daily shall he be praised.
*There shall be **a handful of corn** in the earth upon the top of the mountain;*
the fruit thereof shall shake like Lebanon:
they of the city shall flourish like grass of the earth" Psalm 72:15-16 KJV.

"I have set watchmen upon thy walls,
*O Jerusalem, which shall **never hold their peace***
day nor night;
ye that make mention of the Lord,
keep not silence.
*The Lord has sworn by **His Right Hand**,*
and by the arm of His Strength.
*Surely I will no longer give **thy corn** to be meat for thine enemies;*
and the sons of the stranger shall not drink thy wine,
for which thou has laboured.
But they that have gathered it shall eat it, and praise the Lord;
and they that have brought it together
shall drink it in the courts of my holiness.
Go through, go through the gates,
prepare ye the way of the people;
*cast up, cast up **the highway**;*

gather out the stones;
lift up a standard
for the people.
Behold the Lord hath proclaimed unto the end of the world,
Say ye to the daughter of Zion,
Behold, thy salvation cometh:
behold ***His reward*** *is with him*
and ***His work*** *before him.*
And they shall call them, The ***holy people,***
The ***redeemed*** *of the Lord:*
and Thou shalt be called, sought out,
a city not forsaken."
Isaiah 62:6,8-12 KJV.

I declare that the Lord holds Ireland in His Right Hand,
Like a piece of corn gathered from the harvest,
That will no longer be given over to the enemy.
He has appointed Ireland for His work and His reward,
Ireland is just the corn,
To witness His Hand in action as it moves.
The Lord will make our waters sink into the deep,
And cause the rivers to run like oil[206].

The Watchman has arisen and stands at his post[207],
He stands amidst the darkness and the cold.
At twelve, he hears the sound of the bell,
And the sound broke the silence.
The Watchman awaits the relief of his station,
Or the break of dawn.
A rustle sounds beyond the wall,
But it was just the wind moving a hawthorn bush.

---

206 Ezekiel 32:14 ESV "Then I will make their waters clear, and cause their rivers to run like oil, God."

207 A vision during prayer on the 9th Jan 2019.

He looks down, the light in his lamp is fading,
    But he cannot leave his post to get oil.
Then, lo, a wave arrives and overcomes the full height of the wall,
    Covering him in oil from head to toe.
The Watchman, he will stand on the wall and wait,
    The oil is coming,
        The wave is coming.
Repair the wall, Lord, and lead us,
    Or else the oil will waste away through the cracks.

O ancient city of **Dublin**[208],
    Where the enemy stands like a giant in the land.
I could not come near your wall until the appointed time,
    And at the designated place,
        where I sought your ancient gate[209].
"Reflect upon what I show you,

---

208 Dublin visited on the 26th May 2019.

209 St. Audeon's Church was erected in 1190 and stands close to the medieval centre of the city, but is likely to stand on the location of a much earlier church going back as far as the 7th Century. It is dedicated to St Ouen the 7th century bishop of Rouen and patron saint of Normandy. Adjacent to the church is a park which is significant in that it contains the last surviving original gate to the city, St Audeon's Arch, and a section of the wall dating to at least 1100. It was part of the original wall, but the walls of the city were later extended making this section of the wall internal rather than the perimeter of the city. It is highlighted in orange below. I noticed a small sign which indicated that the park had only reopened on the 14th May, about a week before I felt the burden to come and pray in the city.

go as the wind blows,

do not carry the burdens through the door."

I stand here, Lord, at the place of the watchman,

Upon the last remaining gate

Upon the wall and wait,

And listen for Your Words.

The sounds of the past are drowned out.

My people, Lord, have not learned.

What, my Lord, will turn them to You?

Shall they hear the cry of the birds,

Or turn away because of a fierce wind?

Shall a loud noise or a warning, make them heed?

O, how I yearn to see my people turn to you!

"If he fathers a son who is violent, a shedder of blood,

who does any of these things

(though he himself did none of these things),

who even eats upon the mountains,

defiles his neighbour's wife,

oppresses the poor and needy,

commits robbery,

does not restore the pledge,

lifts up his eyes to the idols,

commits abomination,

lends at interest, and takes profit;

shall he then live?

He shall not live. He has done all these abominations;

he shall surely die; his blood shall be upon himself"

Ezekiel 18:10-13 ESV.

"And I will make this city a horror,

a thing to be hissed at.

Everyone who passes by it will be horrified

and will hiss because of all its wounds.

And I will make them eat the flesh of their sons

and their daughters,
and everyone shall eat the flesh of his neighbour
in the siege and in the distress,
with which their enemies
and those who seek their life afflict them" Jeremiah 19:8-9 ESV.

A sound goes forth,
A new sound must go out over the wall.
But in silence, I walked from that place,
Past Christ Church, and I passed a piece of wall
Where Fagan's Tower once stood,
Also known as the 'watchtower'[210].
Drawn by the Lord in the direction of the State,
To see a sorry state,
But I did not know why I had come here.
Walking around the Castle grounds, seeing the space for the first time,
I remembered that they had celebrated an abomination here.
It was not until I went home that I realised
That it had been a year to the date of that event.
O Lord, have mercy on us,
For the people gathered to express joy
In the death of a generation.

Ireland is like a man floating down the river,
And got its foot stuck on the muddy bank[211].
The resistance of the flow,
Caused the man to spin around and face the other way.
The foot caught in the muddy bank,
Stirred up the sediment and caused the water to lose clarity.

---

210 Clanfagan (2019) 'Fagan's gate revisited' [Online] https://clanfagan.com/research/castles-of-the-fagans/fagan-s-gate-revisited

211 A vision during a time of prayer on the Dec 15th 2018

O the foolishness in the youth of my nation,
Not doing what is right,
And instead, doing what was known to be wrong[212].
A nation who should have sought God about the 'system'
Rather than acting in rebellion.
One who should have sought good things and good friends,
But instead, they chose mockers,
And so, they fell into lust.
Lord, give us Your Ways and Thoughts,
remove any restrictions preventing breakthrough for Ireland.
Take everything, Lord.
Reveal Your mysteries to us,
And show us who we are as a nation and Your purpose for us.

"The fool has said in his heart there is no God.
They are corrupt, they have done abdominal works,
there is none that doeth good.
The Lord looked down from heaven upon the children of man,
to see if there were any that did understand,
and seek God.
They are all gone aside, they are all together become filthy;
there is none that doeth good, no, not one"
Ps 14:1-3 KJV.

Some have kept the faith here in Ireland,
But it seems we were predestined to learn the hard way.
A nation who had learned of God,
But not how to live a life of worship
[a spiritual life of walking in righteousness].
In its youth, my nation lost out on guidance, companionship, and purpose.
We did not turn to You, Lord,
And seek You for Your Ways to be established in our land.

212 John 1:16 ESV *"For from his fullness we have all received, grace upon grace."*

Lord, restore what was lost, restore Your guidance in our lives,
That we would not lean on our own understanding
But seek Your Will in all matters.
Lord, change our nation so that it once again honours You,
So that Ireland can be a good leader without selfish motives.
Lord, restore any lost purpose, goals,
That You have set out in advance for Ireland.
Restore a healthy fear of You,
Knowing that we can hope and trust in Your Mercy[213].
In the scroll of the book, what is written of Ireland?[214]

"I waited patiently for the Lord and he inclined unto me,
and heard my cry.
He brought me up also out of the horrible pit,
out of the miry clay and set my feet upon a rock,
and established my goings.
And he hath put a new song in my mouth,
even praise unto our God; many shall see it,
and fear, and shall trust in the Lord"
Psalm 40:1-3 KJV.

Lord, please compensate for our faults
And regain possession of what was lost to time,
The losses and failures have
Occurred because the days are evil[215]!

"Awake thou that sleepest and arise from the dead,
and Christ shall give thee light.
See them that ye walk circumspectly, not as fools,
but as wise, redeeming the time,

---

213 *Psalm 147:11 ESV "but the Lord takes pleasure in those who fear him, in those who hope in his steadfast." love"; Mark 9:23 ESV "And Jesus said to him, ""If you can'! All things are possible for one who believes.'"*

214 *Psalm 40:7 ESV "Then I said, "Behold, I have come; in the scroll of the book it is written of me."*

215 *Ephesians 5:16 ESV "making the best use of the time, because the days are evil."*

because the days are evil.
Wherefore be ye not unwise,
but understanding what the will of the Lord is"
Ephesians 5:14-17 KJV

"Take notice of the wall!"[216]

"The watchmen that went about the city, found me"[217]
The church has been found.
"they smote me, they wounded me"
But there should have been gentleness.
There was no comfort of grace,
wounded by false doctrine.
"the keepers of the walls took away my veil from me"
They took away her modesty,
And did not warn about the enemies,
And made false accusations.

Those who stand watch are 'ministers of the Word'[218]

216 A vision during a time of prayer on the 28th Jan 2019.

217 Song of Solomon 5:7 ESV "The watchmen found me as they went about in the city; they beat me, they bruised me, they took away my veil, those watchmen of the walls."

218 Isaiah 62:6 ESV "On your walls, O Jerusalem, I have set watchmen; all the day and all the night they shall never be silent. You who put the Lord in remembrance, take no rest."

O Ancient stronghold of **Armagh**
Where are your walls?[219]
I cannot go to your walls for they are gone,
And so, I have gone to a secure place where
Its walls are thick, and its tower is high,
Here, people seek the Lord both day and night.
The Lord has given a space to pray,
Where I can look out on the city,
Here I shall wait on the Lord.
"There is swearing, lying, murder,
stealing, and committing adultery;
they break all bounds,
and bloodshed follows bloodshed.
***Therefore the land mourns**, and all who dwell in it languish,*
and also the beasts of the field
and the birds of the heavens,
and even the fish of the sea
are taken away"
Hosea 4:2-3 ESV.

But there is hope:
"For the love of Christ controls us,
because we have concluded this:
that one has died for all,

219 Visited Armagh on the 8th June 2019.

therefore all have died"
2 Corinthians 5:14 ESV.

Then the Lord asked me "look and tell me what you see."
I looked, and I saw two churches in elevated positions.
Their foundations were built upon the ancient stories,
boastful in what was accomplished,
rather than being busy to GO and DO and BE a light.
I saw faded colours, because of the distance.
I saw a cloud above but no rainfall.
I saw houses in their midst but hidden by trees and overgrowth.
The view is not clear.
I saw a quietness, a stillness, no movement, or sound!
Not even the clouds or trees moved.
Then I saw a seed, carried by the wind, go past my window.
'Where will it go? What will grow from it?'
Only the Lord can say.
I see clarity coming, rays of light breaking through,
And a breakthrough in the cloud,
And I hear the sound beat of a new song starting.

I saw a vision of Ireland as if a man,
Floating down the river,
And he snagged his elbow on the riverbank,
Hindering progression[220].
This man began to look towards physical needs,
Rather than the spiritual,
Like a baby with many needs looking for support.
It is as if he was a father,
Who considered leaving the water to care for the child.
'Come and give me what I need' called the child.
He left the river to help and then returned to the river,

---

220 A vision during a time of prayer on the 16th Dec 2019.

And moved on.
Every day that repeated and the child would look for him.
But he should have responded,
'Come with me my child, into the river'.
The child's needs will only be met in the river,
By the father attempting to care for the child in another way,
Only kept the child away from the right source.

"The words of a man's mouth are as deep waters,
and the wellspring of wisdom as a flowing brook"
Proverbs 18:4 KJV.

In the youth of my nation,
Leaders looked to provide physical needs first,
Rather than words and wisdom from God.
Lord, forgive us for our incorrect manner of fatherhood.
I repent of these errors and ask for restoration in our relationship,
Not so that Ireland may leave the river,
But that it would invite others to take a journey
With You.
I exalt You, Lord, for the grace that You have shown to us.
Please continue this work in my nation.
You, Lord, can supernaturally provide in ways that we cannot
comprehend.
You provide for us spiritually first, and then physically.
Yes, You Lord, provide everything we need[221].
You are the bread of life,
And so, we hunger for You.
You protect us[222] and have adopted us into Your family,
You have given us a place to belong[223].

---

221 Such as the Israelites who hungered and were fed, see Exodus 16:1-3.

222 Like when He protected the Israelites from the Pharoah at the Red Sea, Exodus 14:10-12

223 Galatians 4:5-7 ESV "to redeem those who were under the law, so that we might receive adoption as sons. And because you are sons, God has sent the Spirit of his Son into our hearts, crying, "Abba! Father!" So you are no longer

You have given our lives meaning[224],
Leading us by the Spirit of God with a Kingdom mindset.

Then I had a vision of a flower,
It was growing on top of the wall[225].
It was laden with seed,
And had sprouted in a peculiar place.
It had a brown centre, yellow petal, and green leaves.
An enemy lurks beyond the wall,
Faceless, walking just beyond sight.
Into the shadows of darkness,
I saw the seed go forth
and it took root beyond the wall,
bringing light.
The light was keeping the enemy further away,
And yet spreading again,
And again, keeping the enemy away.
An army of flowers in search of light,
Are pushing back the shadows and the darkness.

---

a slave, but a son, and if a son, then an heir through God."

224 Psalm 138:8 ESV "The Lord will fulfill his purpose for me; your steadfast love, O Lord, endures forever. Do not forsake the work of your hands."

225 A vision during a time of prayer on the 19th Feb 2019.

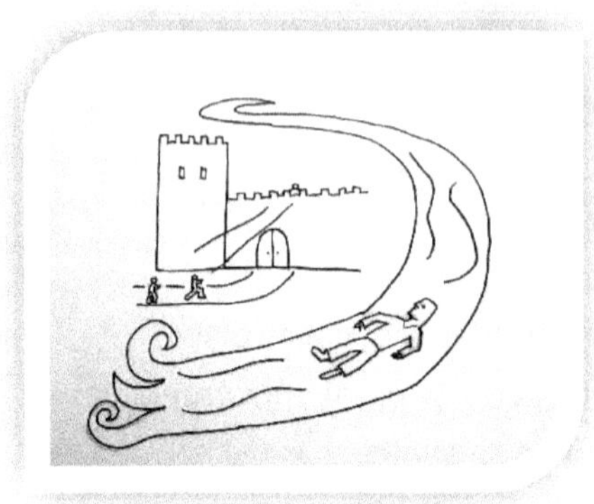

O ancient city of **Limerick**,
Where the invaders settled in strength,
Making a base to spread across the land[226].
Here a stronghold was made stronger and stronger
But the siege of rebellion overcame it.
I have come to your ancient wall,
And have stood upon the watchtower
And watched the mighty river flowing by.

"The wilderness and the dry land shall be glad;
the desert shall rejoice and blossom like the crocus;
it shall blossom abundantly and rejoice with joy and singing.
The glory of Lebanon shall be given to it,
the majesty of Carmel and Sharon.
They shall see the glory of the Lord,
the majesty of our God.
Strengthen the weak hands, and make firm the feeble knees.
Say to those who have an anxious heart,
"Be strong; fear not!
Behold, your God will come with vengeance,
with the recompense of God.

226 Visited Limerick on the 22nd June 2019.

He will come and save you."
Then the eyes of the blind shall be opened,
and the ears of the deaf unstopped;
then shall the lame man leap like a deer,
and the tongue of the mute sing for joy.
For waters break forth in the wilderness,
and streams in the desert;
the burning sand shall become a pool,
and the thirsty ground springs of water;
in the haunt of jackals,
where they lie down,
the grass shall become reeds and rushes.
And a highway shall be there,
and it shall be called the Way of Holiness;
the unclean shall not pass over it.
It shall belong to those who walk on the way;
even if they are fools, they shall not go astray.
No lion shall be there,
nor shall any ravenous beast come up on it;
they shall not be found there,
but the redeemed
shall walk there"
Isaiah 35:1-9 ESV.

"And you were dead in the trespasses and sins"
Ephesians 2:1 ESV.

"I say this in order that no one may delude you
with plausible [fine sounding arguments] arguments"
Colossians 2:4 ESV.

I declare a word of hope:
Be strong, fear not! Behold, your God will come.
He will come and save you.
Lord God protect the city from "fine-sounding arguments".

Early in the morning will I seek You, Lord
And have 'a touch of a path of the river ahead'[227].
Lock me away
In thy secret place.
Take me deeper still
In the Holy place.
Close me in this room
So that I'll hear Your Voice.
You are very special to me,
A friend indeed, a Saviour,
Worthy O worthy are You, Lord!

Then, I saw Ireland as if a man going down the river,
About to be dipped under the water,
Like a baptism, of fire and water.
In its youth, Ireland had got a baptism of fire,
And was immediately thrown into leadership
And sent out with a message
Of love to those in darkness.
The leadership was not based upon the strength of the nation,
But upon a determination to obey God.
A nation called not just to carry the gifts,
But to be a gift,
And to lead others into a new way of worship.
But Ireland, you have not been baptized in the river,
You have not reached fulfilment,
Where is your vision?
Let your devotion to the Lord, be to pray,
Don't just have a touch of the river, but let it carry you,
Go deeper, and don't get back out!

---

227 A vision during a time of prayer on the 17th Dec 2018.

"Blessed are those whose strength is in you,
in whose heart are the highways to Zion.
As they go through the Valley of Baca [weeping]
they make it a place of springs;
the early rain also covers it with pools"
Psalms 84:5-6 ESV.

Through His Grace, sorrows are changed into blessings,
Surely then the Lord planted me as a tree in the valley of Baca.

"Ah, stubborn children," declares the Lord,
"who carry out a plan, but not mine,
and who make an alliance,
but not of my Spirit, that they may add sin to sin;
who set out to go down to Egypt,
without asking for my direction,
to take refuge in the protection of Pharaoh
and to seek shelter in the shadow of Egypt!
Therefore shall the protection of Pharaoh turn to your shame,
and the shelter in the shadow of Egypt
to your humiliation" Isaiah 30:1-3 ESV.

Ireland did not take counsel with You
And the strength of our sin became a national shame
And we went into confusion!
A drought was on us for my backsliding[228],

---

228 See Jeremiah 14:7-12 ESV "Though our iniquities testify against us, act, O Lord, for your name's sake; for our backslidings are many; we have sinned against you. O you hope of Israel, its savior in time of trouble, why should you be like a stranger in the land, like a traveler who turns aside to tarry for a night? Why should you be like a man confused, like a mighty warrior who cannot save? Yet you, O Lord, are in the midst of us, and we are called by your name; do not leave us." Thus says the Lord concerning this people: "They have loved to wander thus; they have not restrained their feet; therefore the Lord does not accept them; now he will remember their iniquity and punish their sins." The Lord said to me: "Do not pray for the welfare of this people. Though they fast, I will not hear their cry, and though they offer burnt offering and grain offering, I will not accept them. But I will consume them by the sword, by famine, and by pestilence."

And yet,
The Lord
Sustained me
In His Hand.

So, Ireland was open to attack,
the tree planted in the valley was cut down,
and thrown into the river,
it became a log that would continue down the river[229].
The trees were overcome by enemies set upon destruction[230].

"I will give you the treasures of darkness
and the hoards in secret places,
that you may know that it is I, the Lord,
the God of Israel,
who call you by your name"
Isaiah 45:3 ESV.

In a vision, I saw the watchman standing on the wall,
And he saw two runners approaching,
Seeking an audience with the King[231].
They carried news of the battle,
And sad tidings to the King of his son,
Who had gone to death,
A message for the Father's Heart.

---

229 The same log as seen in a vision during prayer in Dec 2012.

230 See 2 Kings 3:18-19 ESV "This is a light thing in the sight of the Lord. He will also give the Moabites into your hand, and you shall attack every fortified city and every choice city, and shall fell every good tree and stop up all springs of water and ruin every good piece of land with stones."

231 A vision during a time of prayer on the 22 Feb 2019.

O ancient city of **Cashel**
Where kings were anointed[232].
For seven hundred years the walls have stood,
Shaped like a heart,
But only a corner survives.

"My heart grew hot within me.
While I meditated, the fire burned;
then I spoke with my tongue:
"Show me, Lord, my life's end and the number of my days;
let me know how fleeting my life is" Psalm 39:3-4 NIV.

This city did not foresee their end,
they did not see how frail they were,
the town was taken,
the walls were broken, and the roof removed
(symbolising the covering being lost and the protection taken away).

"You were bought at a price;
do not become slaves of human beings"
1 Corinthians 7:23 NIV.

232 Visited Cashel on the 13th July 2019.

Listen to the wind
A gust fills the air, touching the trees.
Demons roam here,
Feeding on this ground.
Let Your Light shine!
Let the demons flee
From this place!
Set the hearts of the people
Back to their God.
Let them not be servants of men,
But servants of God
All that remains is a corner
Of their 'heart' walls
I declare that 'a heart of intimacy will be restored'.

I saw Ireland as if a man
Floating down a river,
That was about to go over the edge of a waterfall[233].
Ireland, what was the dream of your youth?
Was it not that twice you would see trouble,
And that you would then go to the edge
And find your destiny?
You have been in darkness, yes,
But the day of your destiny comes!
You were destined to 'go over the edge'[234],
But treasure will come out of the darkness[235],
Like a diamond that is hidden in the depth of the earth
That has been found and brought to the light.

---

233 A vision during a time of prayer on the 18th Dec 2018.

234 Of the waterfall.

235 Isaiah 45:3 ESV "I will give you the treasures of darkness and the hoards in secret places, that you may know that it is I, the Lord, the God of Israel, who call you by your name."

"Listen, my beloved brothers,
has not God chosen those who are poor in the world
to be rich in faith and heirs of the kingdom,
which he has promised to those who
love him?" James 2:5 ESV.

My land has fallen into sickness, and
Into dishonouring the Lord.
Nor does it make way for His intervention.
But surely the Lord has chosen this land,
And my people to go over the edge,
It was surely His plan of correction,
To lead us to our destiny.
So those who loved Ireland,
Saw her go over the cliff,
And disappear into a cloud of confusion,
A shadow of Egypt caused by her sin[236].
Ireland ate the labour of its hands[237].
Perhaps, if you had chosen a different path,
Then the river would have been smooth,
Without a waterfall.
Falling down, it shall break away the lust,
Which would have been our destruction,
Even if one temptation had been avoided,
The next desire would have been acted upon,
The fall was destined.
God's response,
Is that in His Mercy,
He is going to set the captive free[238].

---

236 Isaiah 30:3 ESV "Therefore shall the protection of Pharaoh turn to your shame, and the shelter in the shadow of Egypt to your humiliation."

237 Psalm 128:1-2 ESV "Blessed is everyone who fears the Lord, who walks in his ways! You shall eat the fruit of the labor of your hands; you shall be blessed, and it shall be well with you."

238 Psalm 145:9 ESV "The Lord is good to all, and his mercy is over all that he has made."

A lamentation begins:

Ireland, Ireland, where have you gone?
I saw you down by the river so,
    But then I saw you go.
Arms and feet tucked in,
    Over the top, you did go.
I looked, I searched,
    But found you not,
        Gone beneath the cloud.
When shall you return,
    I need you to come forth
        and lift me up.
Lord, take us with You for it would
    Save us so,
        I want You near.
Be my protection
    Be my guide
        Help me, help me
            Or I might die.
Ireland, Ireland, are you there?
The roar of the waterfall
    Continued loudly,
        No sign, no hope, close the door.
Then I saw a man appear,
    Coming out of the flow.
He looked different,
    A broken and distressed man.
'Ireland', I shouted
    But he could not hear,
        His journey was so.
I rejoice that the Lord has a plan for Ireland,
    A plan for Ireland
        And the lands of its kin.

Lord, please finish the work You have started.

"And I am sure of this,
that he who began a good work in you
will bring it to completion
at the day of Jesus Christ"
Philippians 1:6 ESV.

I saw a vision of a watchman,
Standing upon the wall at night[239].
A strong wind blew,
Turning the watchman to face inwards.
Then, he saw the people going out,
To do wickedness in the darkness.
Shine the Light!
Shine the light into the camp!
And then I saw other watchmen,
who turned a blind eye to the wickedness.
They had been tainted,
And blew out the light in their lamp,
To allow the darkness to cover the wickedness.
What shall I do my Lord?

"Behold, I will send you Elijah the prophet
before the great and awesome day of the Lord comes"
Malachi 4:5 ESV.
"For the eyes of the Lord are on the righteous,
and his ears are open to their prayer.
But the face of the Lord is against those who do evil"

239 A vision during a time of prayer on the 27th Feb 2019.

1 Peter 3:12 ESV.

Oh, ancient city of **Waterford**,
A garrison for invaders on the Celtic Sea[240].
I came to pray at your Watchtower,
And stood at its foundation.
I stood at your foundation and waited upon my Lord,
But I could see that your wall is divided,
These walls are broken, disjointed.

"Their mother has been unfaithful
and has conceived them in disgrace.
She said, 'I will go after my lovers,
who give me my food and my water,
my wool and my linen,
my olive oil and my drink'"
Hosea 2:5 NIV.

Look and see,
For this city,
Is throwing a banquet for Babylon[241].
You have turned away to your lover,

---

240 Visited Waterford city on the 22nd July 2019.

241 Restaurant on the street called 'Babylon'.

The spirit of Babylon is on your streets.
But I declare the path with your lover,
Is at an end.
Repent and fast!
You have not been walking with the groom[242]
Therefore, repent and return to the Lord.

"Then the men who had been sent
returned to the house and found the servant well"
Luke 7:10 NIV.

Then I believed this for the city,
that whenever I return, that I will find it 'well'.

Then, I saw Ireland as if a man
That had gone off the cliff of a waterfall and disappeared[243]
And he curled up like a baby when landing,
And hit a rock and was broken,
And a ripple went out across the water.
Lust is broken,
Perhaps there was no other way
To take it away.
This crisis left consequences.
Trust is broken,
Marriage is forgotten.
Hope is shattered,
Darkness and loneliness have come.
Love has crumbled,

---

242 See Matt 9:15 ESV "And Jesus said to them, 'Can the wedding guests mourn as long as the bridegroom is with them? The days will come when the bridegroom is taken away from them, and then they will fast.'"

243 A vision during a time of prayer on the 19th Dec 2018.

Overcome by the consequences of sin.
The ripple of lust has swept over the ripples made by trust,
hope and love.
And yet, in such brokenness,
Ireland still did not turn to God.
Instead, in shame, Ireland hid away.
In shock Ireland became numb,
And in pain, found solace with a bottle.

“In the same way we also,
when we were children,
were enslaved
to the elementary principles of the world” Galatians 4:3 ESV.
Saying, "I have sinned by betraying innocent blood."
They said, "What is that to us? See to it yourself"
Matthew 27:4 ESV.

A lamentation continued
Submerged deep in the water,
He did not hear nor see,
And when he resurfaced,
His kin were caught in a trap.
Ireland, I cannot hear your voice
The further you move away
Evil seeks to destroy, lie, imprison and corrupt.
Let us go into the river,
After many tears
Such heartache
Such pain
Ripple upon ripple
Damage upon damage.
The ripples keep spreading.
Jesus, please help.

“I will incline my ear to a proverb;

I will solve my riddle to the music of the lyre[244].
But God will ransom my soul from the power of Sheol,
for he will receive me." Selah Psalms 49:4, 15 ESV.

Onlookers who saw Ireland's fall and the result of it,
said the nation was finished,
but God has a plan[245].

In a vision, I saw a watchman
Look at the wall and he saw a breach[246],
It has been damaged.

"Therefore, behold, the Lord is bringing up against them
the waters of the River, mighty and many,
the king of Assyria and all his glory.
And it will rise over all its channels and go over all its banks"
Isaiah 8:7 ESV.

---

244 Riddle or 'dark saying' was expressed in Ireland through songs.

245 See Rom 8:28 ESV "And we know that for those who love God all things work together for good,h for those who are called according to his purpose", and Prov 19:21 ESV "Many are the plans in the mind of a man, but it is the purpose of the Lord that will stand."

246 A vision during a time of prayer on the 4th March 2019.

O Ancient city of **Kilkenny**
The place of rebellion[247].
There is little left of your walls,
Only the gate of the Black friars,
A route to the Black Abbey.
The Black Abbey was built outside the city to avoid disputes,
And yet it was where the Rebel Government met,
And ruled the nation until Cromwell came.
There is sickness at the gate,
The gate to rebellion
The gateway for the rebel government!
The light is not shining here.
Look I see a vision of a black tar-like substance,
Leading from the Abbey to the gate,
It is like an oily sludge,
What can wash this darkness away?

"[The enemy] They will all come and settle in the steep ravines
and in the crevices in the rocks,
on all the thornbushes and at all the water holes"
Isaiah 7:19 NIV.
"Nevertheless, death reigned from the time of Adam

247 Visited Kilkenny on the 4th August 2019.

to the time of Moses[248],
even over those who did not sin
by breaking a command,
as did Adam,
who is a pattern of the one to come"
Romans 5:14 NIV.

"being stationed at the King's Gate on the east,
up to the present time.
These were the gatekeepers
belonging to the camp of the Levites.
Shallum son of Kore, the son of Ebiasaph, the son of Korah,
and his fellow gatekeepers from his family
(the Korahites)
were responsible for guarding the thresholds of the tent
just as their ancestors had been
responsible for guarding
the entrance to the dwelling of the Lord"
1 Chronicles 9:18-19 NIV.

I declare that this Gate of rebellion will lose its name,
And be called the 'King's Gate',
And the city shall be a place of spiritual leadership
for the nation,
Leading by example,
Serving other cities and counties.
Lord, this gate could not keep out the foreign invader,
but Your Kingdom will not fail!

"My tears have been my food day and night,
while people say to me all day long, "Where is your God?"
These things I remember as I pour out my soul:
how I used to go to the house of God

---

248 Rebellion against God leads to death reigning!

under the protection of the Mighty One
with shouts of joy and praise
among the festive throng"
Psalm 42:3-4 NIV.

I see Ireland as if a man
Washed up on the bank of a river[249]
All around the man, I saw insurmountable mountains of
Addiction, depression, brokenness and more,
And the man was stuck there,
Will his journey continue?
A man with nothing has nothing to lose,
On the brink of forfeiting nationhood
In haste and waste.
But I declare that Ireland will lay it all down for Him,
No honour in it,
There is nowhere left to turn.
His Kingdom rules over all[250].
Ireland this is your chance,
If you step away now, it will all be over.
Yes, Ireland has begun to say yes to God,
To allow Him to reach into the deep parts of its heart,
A hard and difficult place,
A place with little hope.
Ireland has begun to walk by the waters, to think and listen.

"For not by their own sword did they win the land,
nor did their own arm save them,
but your right hand and your arm,
and the light of your face,
for you delighted in them"

---

249 A vision during a time of prayer on the 20th Dec 2018.

250 Psalm 103:19 ESV "The Lord has established his throne in the heavens, and his kingdom rules over all."

Psalms 44:3 ESV.

Ireland, you cannot save yourself by good works,
Only in His Hand will you find your purpose.
Find your foundation in Him,
And reach for supernatural life,
Seeking God and Truth.

THY RIGHT HAND!

"You make known to me the path of life;
in your presence there is fullness of joy;
at <u>your right hand</u> are pleasures forevermore"
Psalms 16:11 ESV.

Lord, let there be a season for my nation to look in the mirror,
And reflect upon its choices.
To review life, troubles, choices, heartaches, and associations
With other nations.
Let the people yearn for something better
Than they currently have.
Let the people realise they cannot live without You,
And lay down each of these things at Your Feet,
To halt everything that is not of You.
May they commit their way to You,
Trust in You, because You will then act[251].
To recognize that by their own hands they will fail,
And that they need You.
May they never settle for what man has to offer,
And continue to search for the Lord's ways.
Help us, Lord, I pray.

"The blessing of the Lord makes rich,

---

251 See Psalm 37:5 ESV "Commit your way to the Lord; trust in him, and he will act."

and he adds no sorrow with it" Proverbs 10:22 ESV.

Lord, establish in our hearts a willingness to obey
despite the dangers we may face.
Help us to walk with childlike faith,
You have never failed me
And You won't fail me now.
Enable us to speak boldly,
To be willing to declare the truth,
No matter the cost.
Let the nations say of Ireland,
That we have chosen to listen and obey God.
Even if they throw accusations that our obedience seems dangerous,
There is no danger.
Even if it seems ridiculous to others,
You have a miraculous plan.
You, Lord, established a foundation of faith in the land.
Your ways, as we can't do it.
Only You can bring it to pass.
We will trust in You for each step.

"The Lord God, who gathers the outcasts of Israel, declares,
'I will gather yet others to him
besides those already gathered'"
Isaiah 56:8 ESV.
"They do all their deeds to be seen by others.
For they make their phylacteries broad
and their fringes long" Matthew 23:5 ESV.
"Thus says the Lord: We have heard a cry of panic,
of terror, and no peace" Jeremiah 30:5 ESV.
"Then you will call upon me and come and pray to me,
and I will hear you.
You will seek me and find me,
when you seek me with all your heart.
I will be found by you, declares the Lord,

and I will restore your fortunes
and gather you from all the nations
and all the places where I have driven you,
declares the Lord,
and I will bring you back to the place
from which I sent you into exile"
Jeremiah 29:12-14 ESV.

In a vision, I saw a watchman standing at his post[252],
Waiting in the rain,
Only sheer determination and dedication
Stops him from seeking cover.
Resolved to protect and committed to the cause.

O ancient city of **Newry**,
Who was once a sign[253] of the rising
Faith in the nation[254].
The face of your patron has been displaced,
And so, I see a great unrest within you

252 A vision during a time of prayer on the 5th March 2019.

253 The town of Newry is caused 'yew tree at the head of the strand'. Legend tells us that Patrick planted a yew tree here as a symbol of the growing faith. The tree was destroyed somewhere around 1162.

254 Visited Newry on the 24th Aug 2019.

And the oppression of your people[255]
I see the flag of compromise at your places of worship.
At your banquet hall,
The pulpit has been discarded
But the city needs to hear the Word preached.
The banqueting table is empty,
So, we ask Lord that You will fill it with food
And invite the guests.

"All that the Father gives me will come to me,
and whoever comes to me I will never cast out"
John 6:37 ESV.

In a vision, I saw Ireland as if a man[256],
Seeing the river begin to rise,
And he grabs a log to sit on it
And the log was the nation as it used to be,
Now mostly out of sight and submerged.
The man no longer looked at the mountains,
And began to survey God's work.
I saw the nation begin its restoration as a place
Of saints and scholars,
Scholars who wrote about a rising faith.
Its people were beginning to live by the Spirit, faith not sight,
walking obediently, letting God open doors in His timing,
Hearts burning with fire,
Making humility spread through their whole being,
Putting God first in every aspect of life
Staying on the path and

---

255 See Amos 3:9 ESV "Proclaim to the strongholds in Ashdod and to the strongholds in the land of Egypt, and say, 'Assemble yourselves on the mountains of Samaria, and see the great tumults within her, and the oppressed in her midst."'

256 A vision during a time of prayer on the 21st Dec 2018.

Getting prepared.
The river will lead to a sea of resources[257],
The generals will know the way,
And people around the nation will gather together.
The fire must spread, and those who witness this
Will be blessed to see such things.
Your calling will be relentless, but you will not lack.
You must stand in the deep waters,
Unlimited, unrestricted, and unstructured worship.
Give over your time to God, and yearn for Him,
Praying over each step.
In the harvest
Your lost children shall return,
The Holy Spirit is convicting their hearts.
I see a people abandoning religion,
Because God is calling them closer to His Heart,
Ireland will be a holy land again.
Prodigals returned, families restored, spiritual orphans finding homes,
A transformation of Ireland[258].
Now rather than focusing inwards, the nation was focusing outwards.
The Lord will give coals for the fire,
Convicted by the Holy Spirit for their evil ways,
And then refined in the fire.

"Therefore thus says the Lord God:
Like the wood of the vine among the trees of the forest,
which I have given to the fire for fuel,
so have I given up the inhabitants of
Jerusalem" Ezekiel 15:6 ESV.
"The Lord is my chosen portion and my cup; you hold my lot"
Psalms 16:5 ESV.

257 A vision during a time of prayer in Dec 2012.

258 See Proverbs 18:10 ESV "The name of the Lord is a strong tower; the righteous man runs into it and is safe."

Lord, if the enemy should send people with corrupt motives,
Let them find You and fall into a deep place with You
Set their heart alight with fire
And then bring them home
To carry that fire and pass it onwards.

"We have thought on your steadfast love,
O God, in the midst of your temple" Psalms 48:9 ESV.
"And the foreigners who join themselves to the Lord,
to minister to him, to love the name of the Lord,
and to be his servants,
everyone who keeps the Sabbath and
does not profane it,
and holds fast my covenant"
Isaiah 56:6 ESV.

The Lord will bring to the nation many sojourners,
Passing by, passing through, drawn here by Him.

"Their quiver is like an open tomb; they are all mighty warriors"
Jeremiah 5:16 ESV.
"lest I strip her naked and make her as in the day she was born,
and make her like a wilderness,
and make her like a parched land,
and kill her with thirst" Hosea 2:3 ESV.

The nation must begin all over again.

In a vision, I saw a watchman who had become weary,
And he was leaning on the wall in tiredness,
Just as the disciples struggled to watch and pray
for an hour[259].

---

259 A vision during a time of prayer on the 6th March 2019.

-

O ancient city of **Downpatrick**,
The stronghold on the high place[260].
I went to the high place,
There was a silence,
In a venue built for sound,
A place for worship,
Is now for sojourners.
But I see the eyes that weep their tears,
The five seats of authority await their filling
Under the authority of Christ.
There is a coldness here,
The face is cold.
Again, I say, the five seats will be filled!
These people say their father is above the Lamb.
Restore Your authority here, Jesus.

"Be to me a rock of refuge,
to which I may continually come;
you have given the command to save me,
for you are my rock and my fortress.
Rescue me, O my God, from the hand of the wicked,

260 Visited Downpatrick on the 24th Aug 2019.

from the grasp of the unjust and cruel man.
For you, O Lord, are my hope, my trust,
O Lord, from my youth" Psalms 71:3-5 ESV.

Lord, begin a new sound here
A sound not seeking its own glory
But happy to take a side seat for You.
Dig up the ground Lord,
Dig up the fallow ground!
You make a pathway,
A highway to be cleared,
A promise to be fulfilled,
A nation to be restored.

And I saw Ireland as if a man standing by a river at night,
While others feared the river,
Ireland will find peace there[261].
From the place of free-flowing waters,
I could review man-made structures
And compare and contrast them to my journey.
The Lord has given us deep waters,
A profound resource of never-ending knowledge,
Wisdom, prayer, worship
Which does not burn out or settle.
And the man went to collect wood for the fire,
There were two types of wood,
Softwood and hardwood.
Softwood burns faster and weighs lighter,
Hardwood lasts longer and is heavy.
Weigh my heart, Lord.
May You find it ready to burn,

---

261 A vision during a time of prayer on the 22nd Dec 2018.

To burn for a long time.

"I will drench the land even to the mountains
with your flowing blood,
and the ravines will be full of you"
Ezekiel 32:6 ESV.

Strengthen my FAITH muscles, Lord, to stand firmly for You for Your Glory.

Ireland, follow the Lord,
And be separated from the world,
Free of tradition and religion.
Trust in God, all you people,
Trust in Him alone,
And forgive and be forgiven.
Step into His timing
And embrace humility,
And freedom in prayer and worship.
I declare that Ireland will put aside the traditions and routines
That hold it back.
Rise up Ireland in strength and boldness,
And be a messenger for the Lord.
You have access to an unfathomable resource,
And dreams and visions.
The fire will keep burning.
The structures have been found wanting.

"All who see me mock me; they make mouths at me;
they wag their heads" Psalms 22:7 ESV.
"Day to day pours out speech,
and night to night reveals knowledge" Psalms 19:2 ESV.
"I pour out my complaint before him;
I tell my trouble before him.
When my spirit faints within me, you know my way!

In the path where I walk they have hidden a trap for me"
Psalms 142:2-3 ESV.

"So I went down to the potter's house,
and there he was working at his wheel.
And the vessel he was making of clay was spoiled in the potter's hand,
and he reworked it into another vessel,
as it seemed good to the potter to do"
Jeremiah 18:3-4 ESV.

Lord, You made Ireland the way it is
So that You could reform the nation,
And reveal Your Glory!
Lord, complete Your work in this land.

In a vision, I saw the lamp of a watchman,
The light was dimming[262],
The oil is low,
Help me, Lord.

262 A vision during a time of prayer on the 14th March 2019.

O ancient city of **Lisburn**[263],
A city of continuous burning[264].
Lord, they have gambled with Your Light.
Have mercy Lord,
And reveal their nakedness.
They have "defiled the Lord and committed adultery"[265].
They say, 'come worship,
Hear the bell at six
But do not come to my garden.'
Then they say 'Behold you must leave,
for the gates are being locked,
You cannot enter here!
You cannot go to see the river!'
So, I found the steps by the road
And looked out at the streets where people
Gathered to celebrate rebellion and witchcraft.
I released a sound which echoed through the streets.
Perhaps one day the gate might be reopened
To the river garden where they may feel Your flow once again.
I declare that they will turn back to hear Your Voice again.

---

263 Visited Lisburn on the 24th Aug 2019.

264 In history, the Church was burnt down several times, the original was burnt down during the 1641 rebellion, and then burnt down again in 1707 along with the castle and the town. Then in 1914, Mrs Metge [a suffragette] bombed the church.

265 Jeremiah 3:2-9 ESV "Lift up your eyes to the bare heights, and see! Where have you not been ravished? By the waysides you have sat awaiting lovers like an Arab in the wilderness. You have polluted the land with your vile whoredom. Therefore the showers have been withheld, and the spring rain has not come; yet you have the forehead of a whore; you refuse to be ashamed. Have you not just now called to me, 'My father, you are the friend of my youth—will he be angry forever, will he be indignant to the end?' Behold, you have spoken, but you have done all the evil that you could." The Lord said to me in the days of King Josiah: "Have you seen what she did, that faithless one, Israel, how she went up on every high hill and under every green tree, and there played the whore? And I thought, 'After she has done all this she will return to me,' but she did not return, and her treacherous sister Judah saw it. She saw that for all the adulteries of that faithless one, Israel, I had sent her away with a decree of divorce. Yet her treacherous sister Judah did not fear, but she too went and played the whore. Because she took her whoredom lightly, she polluted the land, committing adultery with stone and tree.

And I saw Ireland as if a man
That is getting into a boat on the river[266]
It followed the path of the river,
Which passed by a large wall,
And upon the wall were words of judgement,
First of the world,
And then of the church.
The boat came to rest by some ruins,
And the man got out there.
No one was there in that place,
But I saw some broken walls in the area.
But what others do not value,
God can open our eyes to appreciate it.

"Many are the plans in the mind of a man,
but it is the purpose of the Lord that will stand"
Proverbs 19:21 ESV.

A test has come,
One of dedication,
Can you stand together in unity?
Lord God, let us hide in Your Counsel,
And not depend upon our own knowledge or wisdom,
Guide me deeper in Your Truth my Lord.
I saw a vision of a butterfly take flight
And there was a lot of smog in the air
That should kill off all butterflies,
And while some fell to the left and the right,
It did not harm this butterfly,
And it was a beautiful thing.

266 A vision during a time of prayer on the 23rd Dec 2018.

"When the disciples reached the other side,
they had forgotten to bring any bread.
Jesus said to them,
'Watch and beware of the leaven
of the Pharisees and Sadducees'" Matthew 16:5-6 ESV.

Watch for spiritual corruption,
Behold, you trust in deceptive words to no avail[267].
The people, they no longer trust in God or His Ways,
His traditions, His Righteousness,
But they are openly choosing to believe lies.
There seems to be nothing for them to gain,
But more destruction.

"And your ancient ruins shall be rebuilt;
you shall raise up the <u>foundations</u> of many generations;
you shall be called the repairer of the breach,
the restorer of <u>streets</u> to dwell in"
Isaiah 58:12 ESV.

I had been brought back to the waste places[268]
Being brought back to the place
Where I was carried away captive.
I was told about the paths,
And to build up the highway of the Lord.
"A combination of millions of interactions
that God planned to perfection before your birth,
to guide you into His arms.
He chose you. He picked you and loved you through all of your life,
and each moment is as a thousand years to Him.
Can we understand His genuine love for us[269]?"

---

267 Jeremiah 7:8 ESV "Behold, you trust in deceptive words to no avail."

268 See Jeremiah 29:14.

269 Harper, M. (2018) 'Seven Words', Revival Well, pg66.

"See? I move my right hand,
do you perceive it?
If I raise my right hand to move you,
then my right hand moves with you[270]."
Ireland is, what God says it is,
Ireland will become what He plans,
And nothing will triumph over that.
Just like a lion, Ireland will awaken, rise and conquer.
Look what God has done.
The flow of the water has ceased,
But God will make it spring forth miraculously.

And in a vision, I saw a watchman standing at his post,
And as he looked out over the wall,
He saw an army gathering to fight,
And to storm the defences of the cities.

270 Harper, M. (2018) 'Seven Words', Revival Well, pg69.

O ancient city of **Cork**,
An old place of trade[271].
Your gate is shut,
But the Lord will make a pathway.
The defences have been laid low,
But the foundation is still present.
Open the gates to thy past
O ancient city,
Where I find your wall submerged,
Broken by the floods.
The fighting city, one who
Defended itself time and time again.
You look back and commemorate
But your remembrance is forgotten.
You have taken your foundation
Built upon God
And buried it!
And yet it remains,
So, you can build on it once again.
Your light has gone out
The power is off.
But I foresee a day
Where the power returns,
Light will illuminate the walls,
The streets and even the trees.

Lord God, send Your Power
Here – to this place.
Shine Your Light
Into the darkness!
Rebuild Your church as
The strength of this city.

---

271 Visited Cork on the 11th Sep 2019.

Reform the rubble!

Ruined, destroyed, weeping in sackcloth,
wailing, crying out, fleeing, lamenting,
withered, nothing left, carried away, only echoes[272].

"But those who wait on the Lord shall renew their strength:
they shall mount up with wings like eagles"
Isaiah 40:31 ESV.
"Sound the trumpet in Gibeah, the horn of Ramah.
Raise the battle cry in Beth Aven, lead on, O Benjamin"
Hosea 5:8 NIV.

Take me down
By Your still waters,
Lead me on Your Path[273].
You give me breath,
And quiet my heart.
As the birds sing amongst the
Mighty trees.
You uproot, and You plant,
So, plant me by your still, deep waters.
Let me reflect upon
Your goodness,

---

272 See Isaiah 15:2-8 ESV "He has gone up to the temple, and to Dibon, to the high places to weep; over Nebo and over Medeba Moab wails. On every head is baldness; every beard is shorn; in the streets they wear sackcloth; on the housetops and in the squares everyone wails and melts in tears. Heshbon and Elealeh cry out; their voice is heard as far as Jahaz; therefore the armed men of Moab cry aloud; his soul trembles. My heart cries out for Moab; her fugitives flee to Zoar, to Eglath-shelishiyah. For at the ascent of Luhith they go up weeping; on the road to Horonaim they raise a cry of destruction; the waters of Nimrim are a desolation; the grass is withered, the vegetation fails, the greenery is no more. Therefore the abundance they have gained and what they have laid up they carry away over the Brook of the Willows. For a cry has gone around the land of Moab; her wailing reaches to Eglaim; her wailing reaches to Beer-elim.

273 A vision during a time of prayer on the 24th Dec 2018.

And the Rock
Where You set my feet.
You bring me into
The open places,
And open my heart to listen
To Your Voice.
Is like the leaves of Autumn
Which were trodden underfoot.
I was like an uprooted plant,
Laying on its side,
No longer upright.
But You Lord, clothed me in
Your righteousness
And gave me a secure foundation
Hear a new sound!
Come forth, O Lion of Judah!
Let me feel the raindrops
From heaven as they fall.
Thank You, Lord
For changing my heart.
Behold the Lion of Judah
Is roaring in
This land.

And I saw a vision of Ireland as if a man,
Floating down the river,
And he had come to the deep pools.
One of peace,
One of the unknown [danger].
You must be at peace to pass by the danger!
Passing into an area where there are deep pools,
The flow is slower, and there is peace to lay in the water,
Relaxed, listening to the natural sounds above,
The birds and the creaking trees.

"For we are not, like so many, peddlers of God's word,
but as men of sincerity, as commissioned by God,
in the sight of God we speak in Christ" 2 Corinthians 2:17 ESV.

"Or do you suppose it is to no purpose that the Scripture says,
'He yearns jealously over the spirit that he has made to dwell in us'?" James 4:5 ESV.

It is easy to desire a safe place,
A place of comfort where there is no risk,
But you do not find peace there,
Only numbness.
Lord God, allow me to live according to Your Words.
Let me honour You, and not be like those who profane Your Name
According to their lustful desires.
Let me be a reflector of Your Truth,
But not one who seems to be an advisor.
Help me, Lord, I pray.
And yet in these deep pools are deep waters,
And one does not know what they contain.
There is danger there perhaps?
Those who risk those deep places may benefit or may not.
There is a risk.
But some are willing to be forerunners, no matter the cost.
A time is coming where the brothers can walk together again.
Then I began to hear a lament for the religiousness of people,
For the lost, for the inaction of the church, for evil doings.
I saw that the church needed to wake up,
To shed their ways which have kept the Holy Spirit at a distance
And filled their ceremonies
With a lack of intimacy.
Once again, I had a vision of freedom in worship.
Without God, there is no Kingdom seed.

The tradition of silencing freedom
Has left people at the insufficient well of mankind.
There was a call from God for the church to prepare itself.

"Let us rejoice and exult and give him the glory,
for the marriage of the Lamb has come,
and his Bride has made herself ready"
Revelation 19:7 ESV.

And in a vision, I saw a watchman going to the wall,
But he did not know where to stand on the wall[274].
Then he was told to stand on the wall,
At the place where the church meets the wall.
He asked 'Why, Lord?'
But he must do as the Lord commands,
Just as Jeremiah hid his girdle[275]

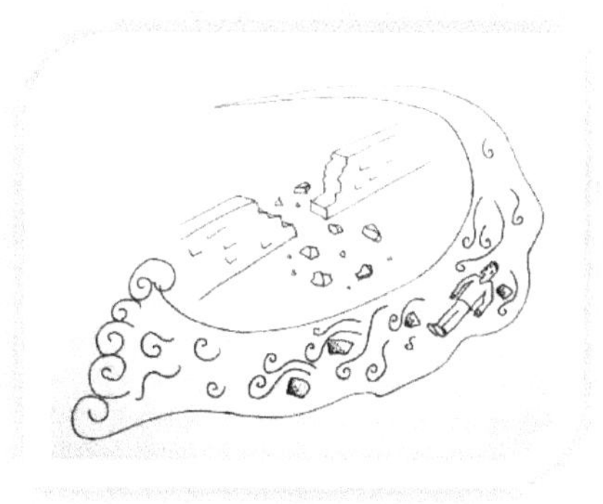

274 A vision during a time of prayer on the 4th April 2019.

275 Jeremiah 13:3-6 ESV "And the word of the Lord came to me a second time, 'Take the loincloth that you have bought, which is around your waist, and arise, go to the Euphrates and hide it there in a cleft of the rock.' So I went and hid it by the Euphrates, as the Lord commanded me. And after many days the Lord said to me, "Arise, go to the Euphrates, and take from there the loincloth that I commanded you to hide there."

O ancient city of **Belfast**,
At the mouth of the Farset[276].
You are sinking, and you have turned
To the Southeast
But perilous waters are near
And you could be gone in just a night[277] .
Where is your river gone?
How had it gone from sight?
Your voice is swallowed up
Your mouth is silent.
A place of commerce has become a cesspit,
Waste floats in your waters.
I declare a day that you turn
To trust in the Lord
And not in mankind
For in Him there is everlasting strength.
Lord, this clock is on reclaimed land,
But that claim is upon sinking land.
I declare Your claim on this land, a claim built upon rock[278].

And I saw Ireland as if a man
Going down the river[279],
And he led the way across the rapids,
A leader to show the way.

---

276 Visited Belfast on 25th Aug 2019. The name Belfast likely originates from the name 'mouth of the farset'. The farset River is a tributary of and where it joins is thought to be where the town originally developed. This location is now called Donegall Quay. Interestingly the Albert Memorial Clock is built upon 'reclaimed land' from the Farset. The clock has been sinking.

277 See Isaiah 15:1-2 ESV "Because Ar of Moab is laid waste in a night, Moab is undone; because Kir of Moab is laid waste in a night, Moab is undone. He has gone up to the temple, and to Dibon, to the high places to weep; over Nebo and over Medeba Moab wails. On every head is baldness; every beard is shorn"

278 Ibid.

279 A vision during a time of prayer on the 25th Dec 2018.

"and the king will desire your beauty.
Since he is your Lord, bow to him"
Psalms 45:11 ESV.

Lord God, draw my family deep into worship,
Let it be our desire.
Every day,
Night upon night,
For no more reason than to rest in Your Presence.
Give us the momentum and the stamina to stay with You
Until the race is run,
Until we come before You.
Lord, fill our homes with the sound of worshippers seeking You.

"Moab is laid desolate...
...I will water thee with my tears...
...and gladness is taken away, and not out of the plentiful field[280]*"*
"The word of the Lord came to me" Jeremiah 16:1 ESV.

Ireland, the time has come to worship in Spirit and Truth,
Keeping the temple clean,
Bringing sacrifice to the altar,
And to be changed in worship.
Freedom! Freedom in the Holy Spirit.
Lord, only You can do it,
To ignite a hunger in our hearts,
A flame that will not go out,
With a like-mindedness to seek You,
To not be content with the normal,
To see Your Kingdom come
And Your Will established in this place.

---

280 See Isaiah 15 & 16.

Only You can do it, Lord, and we are willing servants,
Allow it Lord to bubble up from within our hearts
And overflow into these streets!
Let there be weeping and tears as we seek the Father.
Fill our time with You!
Fill our minds with you!
Fill our hearts with a desire for you.
As for me and my family, we will serve the Lord!

And in a vision, I saw a watchman,
Take notice that the wall has taken damage![281]

And behold, the man clothed in linen,
with the writing case at his waist,
brought back word, saying,
"I have done as you commanded me"
Ezekiel 9:11 ESV.

Lord, the wall has taken damage and needs repair,
It has even reached the path.
Please help, Lord!

281 A vision during a time of prayer on the 10th April 2019.

O ancient city of **Clogher**,
Where people brought idolatry into the church[282].

"You said in your heart, 'I will ascend to heaven;
above the stars of God I will set my throne on high;
I will sit on the mount of assembly
in the far reaches of the north"
Isaiah 14:13 ESV.
"You only have I known of all the families of the earth;
therefore I will punish you for all your iniquities.
"Do two walk together, unless they have agreed to meet?"
Amos 3:2-3 ESV.

Here in this city,
Christianity and paganism chose to walk together.
They brought the gold stone into the church,
Mixing it with their faith.
Lord, forgive us for bringing an idol and paganism into Your House,
Whether for the attention or fame or something else
We have taken an unholy thing into Your sanctuary.
So here I have found no wall,

282 Visited Clogher on the 20th Sept 2019.

No protection because You will not honour such behaviour.
Lord, remove the stench from the wall,
From the foundation here for it is a detestable thing.
Establish Your Light.
Establish clarity.
Establish Your Righteousness.
They are so busy – and in such danger.
They speed along not looking where they are going,
Not realising how close death is to their door.
Wake up! Wake up and see and turn from the danger.
I proclaim that they will turn, and they will turn just in time.
Let the voice of the bride call out and turn them from their ways.
Then the danger will be averted.

And I saw Ireland as if a man travelling down a river,
And the river came to a flood plain[283],
And the man felt a breath of fresh air [from the sea].
A new generation shall enter.
As I looked back up along the river,
I saw that the river, the journey, the calling, became a robe,
The train of His Robe filled the temple[284].
Oh Lord, take me into Your flood plain,
Give me a fresh breath of life from the Holy Spirit,
Spirit fall down on this place.
Fill the hearts of many, my Lord.
Fill the hearts of a new generation for Your Glory[285]!
May Your Glory fill the temple of our hearts.
The train of Your Robe is the river [journey] of my heart.

---

283 A vision during a time of prayer on the 26th Dec 2018.

284 See Isaiah 6:1 ESV "In the year that King Uzziah died I saw the Lord sitting upon a throne, high and lifted up; and the traina of his robe filled the temple."

285 See Psalm 100:5 ESV "For the Lord is good; his steadfast love endures forever, and his faithfulness to all generations"

Be glorified my Papa, my Father, for all that You have done in my heart. Be glorified, be glorified, my King.

"In the year that King Uzziah died I saw the Lord
sitting upon a throne,
high and lifted up;
and the train of his robe
filled the temple.
Above him stood the seraphim.
Each had six wings: with two he covered his face,
and with two he covered his feet, and with two he flew.
And one called to another and said:
"Holy, holy, holy is the Lord of hosts;
the whole earth is full of his glory!"
And the foundations of the thresholds
shook at the voice of him who called,
and the house was filled with smoke"
Isaiah 6:1-4 ESV.

His people carry His Glory
The earth was filled with His Glory.
His train [hem] filled the
Temple of their hearts,
The hem where a woman
Was once healed.

And behold, a woman who had suffered
from a discharge of blood
for twelve years came up behind him
and touched the fringe of his garment,
for she said to herself,
"If I only touch his garment, I will be made well."
Jesus turned, and seeing her he said,
"Take heart, daughter; your faith has made you well."
And instantly the woman was made well.

And when Jesus came to the ruler's house
and saw the flute players
and the crowd making a commotion, he said,
"Go away, for the girl is not dead but sleeping."
And they laughed at him.
When he entered the house, the blind men came to him,
and Jesus said to them, "Do you believe that
I am able to do this?"
They said to him, "Yes, Lord."
Then he touched their eyes, saying,
"According to your faith be it done to you."
And their eyes were opened. And Jesus sternly warned them,
"See that no one knows about it."
But the Pharisees said,
"He casts out demons by the prince of demons."
And Jesus went throughout all the cities and villages,
teaching in their synagogues
and proclaiming the gospel of the kingdom
and healing every disease and every
affliction.
When he saw the crowds, he had compassion for them,
because they were harassed and helpless,
like sheep without a shepherd.
Then he said to his disciples, "The harvest is plentiful,
but the labourers are few;
therefore pray earnestly to the Lord of the harvest
to send out labourers
into his harvest"

Matthew 9:20-24, 28-30, 34-38 ESV.

We are saved by faith and not religion.
The church is asleep, not dead, and Jesus can awaken the church.
Faith opens the eyes.
Religious people throw accusations.
Jesus can heal every disease.

The harvest is His, just pray for labourers.
Then Ireland will enter a season of hearing about the harvest.
A storm is coming, so gather in the harvest.
I saw a vision of the garden of the Lord.
There is an uprooting and replanting of the remnant,
Planting the new seed in a new earth,
Paying the price for faith.
Judgement is coming, wake up! Be holy and dedicated.
Watch for intercessors wailing as if in childbirth,
That is when the movement will begin.
The wedding feast!
The Lord is coming back soon.

And I saw a vision of the watchman
Who had taken notice of the damaged wall[286],
And he banged his fist down on the wall in authority,
And the wall was repaired miraculously.

286 A vision during prayer on the 11th April 2019.

O ancient city of **Derry**,
The one who was not taken or broken[287].
The seven gates,
The fourteenth city
Intact, untaken, the maiden city.
I have come to the fountain
Where fresh water shall come,
Where people will come to draw that water.
Open the gateways between
The north and the south
Through this place
Which was owned by both North and South[288].
In this city
Unity will come!
And lead unity North and South
To other cities across this land

"Why do you cry out over your hurt?
Your pain is incurable.
Because your guilt is great,
because your sins are flagrant,
I have done these things to you" Jeremiah 30:15 ESV.
"Woe to him who gets evil gain for his house,
to set his nest on high,
to be safe from the reach of harm!
You have devised shame for your house by
cutting off many peoples;
you have forfeited your life.
For the stone will cry out from the wall,
and the beam from the woodwork respond.
For the earth will be filled with the knowledge
of the glory of the Lord

287 Visited Derry on the 22nd Sep 2019.

288 The city was once part of Donegal and is now part of Derry.

as the waters cover the sea"
Habakkuk 2:9,10-11, 14 ESV.

Forgive us, Lord, and help us to rebuild,
Not a nation founded on an unjust gain,
But one built for Your Glory!
Strongholds are broken
The Lord rebuilds!!!
Hearts are crushed
The Lord rebuilds!!!
A fractured nation
The Lord rebuilds!!!
Lord God, let my people know freedom in You.
They have been divided, with their backs
To one another but
Now brought together
For Your Glory.

And I saw Ireland as if a man
Who had come down the river to the sea[289]
Then I saw the rain falling, dams breaking,
From the flood plains into the sea.
There was a change from a little depth in freshwater
To an immense depth in saltwater [salt of the earth[290]].
Saline brings healing.
Some people got snagged on debris,
But a tsunami wave will hit and free them all.
I saw in a vision other people stuck in the flood pains
And unable to get to the sea,
A battle began in deep places

289 A vision during a time of prayer on the 27th Dec 2018.

290 Matthew 5:13 ESV "You are the salt of the earth, but if salt has lost its taste, how shall its saltiness be restored? It is no longer good for anything except to be thrown out and trampled under people's feet."

And I shouted back towards land
All those people heard and understood.
There was a change from freshwater to saltwater.

"Now the men of the city said to Elisha,
'Behold, the situation of this city is pleasant,
as my Lord sees, but the water is bad, and the land is unfruitful.'
He said, "Bring me a new bowl, and put salt in it."
So they brought it to him.
Then he went to the spring of water and threw salt in it and said,
'Thus says the Lord, I have healed this water;
from now on neither death nor miscarriage shall come from it.'
So the water has been healed to this day,
according to the word that Elisha spoke"
2 Kings 2:19-22 ESV.

A change in depth: while a river can be deep,
The sea is gigantic, a resource that cannot be consumed,
It casts waves upon the land,
And rain upon the mountain.
And yet while we waited for messages to get through,
A massive tsunami hit the land,
Freeing those who were stuck
And carried them out to sea.
It also delivered a depth to the river,
Combined with rain caused a pressure which broke the dams!
Which, in turn, caused an even greater flood across the land.
Judgement is coming to the world,
The end approaches.
The Babylon spirit, the adulterous hearts, the apostate church,
Shall all be judged.
But there is a rise of a new generation.
Oh remnant, go high, with new clarity, love, truth, holiness.

Behold a cloud of rain comes, a new birth, and a new wave.
The Lord has been doing a deep restoration[291]
So, adopt those who are in grief
Over the detestable things being done.
Declare a time to weep, weeping at the well, a river of tears, a request for light[292].

"I am the Lord your God,
who stirs up the sea so that its waves roar—
the Lord of hosts is his name" Isaiah 51:15 ESV.

There are three swords.
A new mantle for the awakened Church[293],
And a new heart towards prodigals.

In a vision, I saw a watchman stand at his post,
And he took up in his hand a shofar,
And released a song from the watchtower,
The sound went beyond the wall.
The enemy has been spotted and will be met in battle!
The sound notifies the people to gather,
To defend, to look beyond, to hear and pay attention.
A new song is heard!
It declares that there are those of faith on the wall,
And they are taking a stand in the spiritual realm.

291 Like Jeremiah in the mire [Jer 38:6].

292 See Isaiah 51.

293 See Isaiah 58:1-12.

The Mountain

In a vision, I saw the Lord holding out his hand to me[294].
'Lord, I'm scared' I said in response.
And I looked up and saw a white snow-topped mountain
and He said, 'this is a holy place.'
Over streams, He led me,
Along a path, He led me,
Through the trees of a forest, He led me,
I heard the wind touch the branches.
Through a stony brook
He led me,
I was barefoot, and
My feet were washed clean.
Across slippery rocks
He helped me.
When my strength failed me,
He carried me
To the edge of the snow.
'Where do I go?' I asked.
'What do I do?' I asked.
So, I lay down on the snow
And looked up,
And He showed me the sky
And the clouds, and
Beyond that into space
And to see even mysteries
Of the universe.
He gave me sight to see
Beyond my comprehension,
'Now climb higher' He said.
With every step, the snow

294 A vision during a time of prayer on the 29th December 2018, at 7 hour prayer event in Dublin.

Swallowed me deeper,
It demanded more of me,
'take it all, Lord'.
And when all strength was gone,
He lifted me up, and we
Walked on the snow
His light bright and shining
Like the sun
It was so bright that I could not look.
And so, I closed my eyes,
'Let me be your sight' He said
And so, I walked on and
Listened to His Voice only,
There was nothing else!

"And if a man strive for mysteries
Yet is he not crowned
Except he strive lawfully" 2 Timothy 2:5 KJV.
"The Lord is the portion of mine inheritance
And of my cup,
Thou maintainest my lot" Psalm 16:5 KJV.

To understand a mystery is to receive a crown.
I walked on further,
And then from the snow onto white rock,
Sheared white by His Holiness,
then at the peak,
He spat into mud
And opened my sight.
I saw the land below,
Shimmer in green,
and He said to
Me 'speak' and I said
My words are so unholy, but
He beckoned me to speak,

So, I said: 'Repent for the Kingdom of God is near'.
Then I saw a shaking begin and the
Ground broke open and was divided,
And from within the divide,
I saw diamonds coming forth,
Then there was not just one or two
But many came forth to stand
In the gap.
Light irradiated the diamonds,
And it emitted
A light as clear as crystal.
And I saw one diamond
That had turned blue
I asked 'What is this diamond?'
And then I knew it was
A new generation of intercessors rising up!

"the gates thereof languish;
They are black unto the ground;
And the cry of Jerusalem is gone up.
And their nobles have sent their little ones to the waters:
They came to the pits and found no water;
They returned with their vessels empty;
They were ashamed and confounded,
And covered their heads.
Because the ground is chapt,
For there is no rain in the earth,
The plowmen were ashamed,
They covered their heads"
Jeremiah 14:2-4 KJV.

Lord have mercy upon this generation.

"He will turn again he will have compassion upon us;
He will subdue our iniquities,
And thou wilt cast all their sins
Into the <u>depth of the sea</u>"
Micah 7:19 KJV.

"I thank thee O Father,
Lord of heaven and earth,
Because thou hast hid these things
From the wise and prudent,
And hast revealed them unto babes"
Matthew 11:25 KJV.

"The Lord God is my strength,
And he will make my feet like hinds feet,
And he will make me to walk upon <u>mine high places</u>"
Habakkuk 3:19 KJV.

Now, *"go stand in the gate of the children[295]"*.
There will be a *"wall of fire round about"* and *"glory in the midst"[296]*.

And I lifted my eyes and saw, and behold, four horns!
And I said to the angel who talked with me, "What are these?"
And he said to me, "These are the horns that have scattered Judah,
Israel, and Jerusalem."
And I said, "What are these coming to do?"
He said, "These are the horns that scattered Judah,
so that no one raised his head.
And these have come to terrify them,
to cast down the horns of the nations
who lifted up their horns
against the land of Judah to scatter it"
Zechariah 1:18-19, 21 ESV.

---

295 Jer 17:8 ESV "He is like a tree planted by water, that sends out its roots by the stream, and does not fear when heat comes, for its leaves remain green, and is not anxious in the year of drought, for it does not cease to bear fruit."

296 See Zech 2:5. "Wall of fire" can also be seen as a 'ring of fire' a wall of protective fire.

The Lord had sent His servants,
To remove the horns of judgement from the nations,
And to release a new sound
And to allow for reconciliation for my land.
But the way was hidden[297]
And the steps are twisted
And the house is broken.
So, they asked 'Gatekeeper, may we enter?'
Then oil was poured out on the gate
And the gate was opened.
There are seven steps, where the oil is poured out.
And I looked, and I saw a tree
Its trunk had been severed,
It had many scars,
And its roots had been cut.
And again, the oil is poured out.
I went to see what man had made
It was on the land of the house
And made higher than it.
It was an idol that had brought destruction to the house.
"I will sprout up a tree higher than what mankind
Has built and it will overshadow what man
Has done in this land."
Truth shall fall like acid,
melting away the stones of idolatry.
And the tree that sprouts up,
It is the rise of the 'Joshua generation'[298]

---

297 A difficult place to find in County Meath – undisclosed.

298 Joshua 11:13-16 ESV "But none of the cities that stood on mounds did Israel burn, except Hazor alone; that Joshua burned. And all the spoil of these cities and the livestock, the people of Israel took for their plunder. But every person they struck with the edge of the sword until they had destroyed them, and they did not leave any who breathed. Just as the Lord had commanded Moses his servant, so Moses commanded Joshua, and so Joshua did. He left nothing undone of all that the Lord had commanded Moses. So Joshua took all that land, the hill country and all the Negeb and all the land of Goshen and the lowland and the Arabah and the hill country of Israel and its lowland"

The Joshua generation will have their own stones
And they will point to Christ.
And I called out to the Lord's servants,
Go to the window and tell me of the state of the house
[the church].
And they replied
The song is broken
They have left their first love.
Freedom is gone
The bell is broken
The church longs to come back.
It was given the gift of dance
But has stopped dancing.
Then they called the dance back:
Dancers rise up[299]
The light will surround you
And you will sing and dance with greater joy.
And they also saw old worm-like vines
But God will destroy the overgrown weeds [cares of this world].
She is like a woman abandoned
That has not been loved.
Ireland, it is time to rise up to your true identity
Pour wine and oil
Over the bride to heal her.
Now is a time of healing
Like a woman laying down
Who seems as if lifeless
But there is life and healing taking place.
And I saw a procession coming through the church
With a sound of brokenness
Then I saw another procession coming through the church
With a new sound.
And in the hearth, there was oil and a dove,

---

299 The need for the Irish to start dancing again was also highlighted at the Bangor conference, June 2019.

A harp and a sound,
And the Word watched over the doorway
As the dancers danced with banners.
The uncut stones were anointed with oil.
And I saw Ireland
Like a man who had been on his knees
And intercessors had come to pray for him.
And they anointed his feet
And lifted him to his feet
Rising up to a kingly status and authority
To declare, rule and reign.
And then a crowd of people
Came to the hill of the King in joy.

Limerick

And I went to the place where my nation caused its brother pain[300]

"Gird your sword on your thigh,
O mighty one, in your splendor and majesty!
In your majesty ride out victoriously
for the cause of truth and meekness and righteousness;
let your right hand teach you awesome deeds!"
Psalms 45:3-4 ESV.

And the trail led to the door number eighteen[301]
Which was long closed.
And then, the Lord opened it
A remnant of those who were hurt
They have not let go of their heritage.
Life! New life![302]

---

300 Visit to Limerick again, on the 17th August 2019.

301 Wolfe Tone Street, Limerick.

302 Symbolised by the meaning of 18.

Then onwards to the place of hurt[303]
To hear a song of lament and change.
Able men shall now rise from this place
Responsible for ministering in the house of God[304].
Lead me to Your river,
Where we can meet.
Only You can bring healing at the river Lord
To see the oil being poured out
And forming a ring of blue fire
In the water.

303 Redemptorist church.

304 1 Chronicles 9:13 ESV "besides their kinsmen, heads of their fathers' houses, 1,760, mighty men for the work of the service of the house of God."

ISRAEL
CHAPTER 10

"Who has purposed this against Tyre,
the bestower of crowns,
whose merchants were princes,
whose traders were the honoured of the earth?"
Isaiah 23:8 ESV

O Israel my brother,
Will I now come to you?
I have sought the Lord,
And I had a vision of a watchman,
And in his hand was a flaming sword,
And he was travelling at speed[305].
Then he drove the sword downwards into the ground,
And yet continued to travel at speed,
Now turning slightly and making a circle,
A circle of flaming fire seared
Into the soil.
And then, in another vision[306],

---

305 A vision during prayer on the 28th Jun 2019.

306 Ibid.

I saw a very striking blue water
Coming through a cave,
And on the ceiling of the cave,
I saw diamonds,
A treasure to be uncovered.
And I was also reminded of another vision,
From a long time ago,
A vision of Abraham's well
And into my hand was placed a leaf
Which was a message from the Lord.
And yet another vision,
Of thunder, lightning, and rain[307],
The Lord's Glory will be evident
'As the thunder sounds overhead'.

I will show you the foundations of the city,
And the names of the apostles on them[308].
Every change must be established by the evidence
Of two or three witnesses[309].
I have made you this day a fortified city and an iron pillar,
And bronze walls against the whole land.
They shall fight against you,
But they shall not [finally] prevail against you,
For I am with you[310].
Lord, You have been opening the highway,
You have sent the children of my land[311],
To heal us and send us on our way
So that we might hear the bell ring once again

---

307 A vision during prayer on the 29th Jun 2019.

308 See Rev 21.

309 2 Cor 13:1 ESV "This is the third time I am coming to you. Every charge must be established by the evidence of two or three witnesses."

310 See Jeremiah 1:19.

311 Bangor conference June 2019, Norweigan intercessors came to Ireland to repent.

All across the land.

You and only You Lord, have stirred up the hearts of many,
To take a journey to Israel,
And You have stirred my very core.
I hear a lament,
A deep lament from my land,
Weeping like a father in grief for a son,
A sound that cannot be contained,
Nor even replicated
Unless the Lord enables me.
The brothers, they stand apart,
And the doors are shut[312].
And yet I know that I must go to the trees[313],
For my brother planted the trees
Who resides in my land[314].
The fire of the enemy has poisoned the minds
Of the people, and they shout hatred at my brother[315].
And so, the fire has fallen from the sky,
And has been burning the trees which had been planted[316].
I have found rotten roots at the tree of our nation,
Life must return to these roots,
Reconciliation between Ireland and Israel is vital[317]
Only Jesus can do it.
I have made that journey,

---

312 The door of the church, and the door of Zionism are shut to one another, seen during a time of worship in Basel Switzerland, 2017.

313 KKL (2016) '50th Anniversary Celebration of the Eamon De Valera Forest' [Online] http://www.kkl-jnf.org/about-kkl-jnf/green-israel-news/november-2016/eamon-de-valera-forest-50-years-galilee/ Nov 8 2016.

314 The 10,000 trees were bought by the Jewish community in Ireland as a gift to De Valera.

315 The rise of Anti-Israeli politics and media in Ireland.

316 The fire bombs from Palestine.

317 See Zech 14 and Mal 4.

And have gone up to Jerusalem[318].
And yet I cannot find my way,
For the roads have been closed
And I cannot get to my resting place[319].
Only the Lord can do this thing,
Only He can find a path where there is no path.
When all hope is gone, He makes a pathway,
He guides me to the meeting place,
A crossing that I must pass.
Even if my resting place had been before my eyes,
I would not have found it,
Unless the Lord had directed me.
Lord, You have brought me to a place of sustenance,
And have prepared a banqueting table.
You lead me beyond the Damascus Gate,
And along Your Path[320].
You are the shade at my right hand,
And You lead me to rest and wait upon You.
You gather Your servants from distant lands,
And bring them here to meet with You,
And to present a petition of their hearts and their land.
And as I prayed by the wall[321],
I saw a vision of rocks being formed in the depths of the earth,
Created for a purpose,
You have declared:
'My temple shall be made of uncut stones'.
You lead me to the garden,
And sit me down under an almond tree
And speak tenderly to me of Your plans.

---

318 Arrived in Israel on the 13th October 2019.

319 Arrived during Sabbath and many roads in Jerusalem centre were closed by the Orthodox Jews and so I could not easily locate my hotel.

320 Via De La Rosa.

321 A time of prayer at the Western Wall in Jerusalem 14th Oct 2019.

And in a vision a doorway that leads to tree[322],
And then I saw the wall once again,
And forming out of the joins in the wall,
Words began to come into sight,
But they were written in Hebrew
And I could not understand them.
Then the words were gone
And I saw different colours of gold dust
Begin to pour out of the wall.
You lead me on to a high place[323],
From there I saw the ancient city.
You go ahead of Your servants again and again,
And open up a space, and time of worship,
And only You Lord could have done it[324].
I declare a time of intimacy over Jerusalem,
A give a gift[325] to remind the bride of the groom.
A song has gone forth to welcome the rain[326].
And just like Jesus, I met with the twelve,
And leaving a place near King David's tomb,
We left the city walls and headed for Gethsemane
With torches in our hands.
And I looked to my right as I descended into the valley,
And I saw a flash of light in the sky,
And then more bursts of light
And the sounds of thunder.
A storm was rolling in, with lightning striking the ground,
And moving across the sky,
And then the gentle caress of rain

---

322 A vision during prayer at a garden near the Jaffa Gate, Jerusalem, October 14th 2019.

323 20th floor prayer room.

324 Worship slot programmed for 'Ireland' even though it had not been arranged.

325 A scarlet scarf.

326 The song 'let it rain'.

as it fell from the sky[327].
The sound of thunder rolled across the sky,
A roar in the air as I looked upon the Lion's Gate
From the valley below.
There is no rest for the watchman in Jerusalem,
Even at night, he awakes to seek Your Face,
And goes out to a place to meet You.
And in the daytime,
The believers gather from afar,
And dance a sing with banners,
They speak of the crown,
And of oil and wine.
And when I think of those words that I cannot know,
Even those You reveal to me[328],
What words can express this wonder?

"And I saw the holy city, new Jerusalem,
coming down out of heaven from God,
prepared as a bride adorned for her husband.
And I heard a loud voice from the throne saying,
"Behold, the dwelling place of God is with man.
He will dwell with them,
and they will be his people,
and God himself will be with them as their God"
Rev 21:2-3 ESV.

It shall come to pass in the latter days
that the mountain of the house of the Lord
shall be established as the highest of the mountains,
and shall be lifted up above the hills;

---

327 Fulfilment of the vision of rain and thunder which the Lord weeks before the journey, and the fulfilment of the song that had been sung in the high place.

328 The day after my vision, at a gathering, I met a prophetic artist who had seen and painted the Western Wall with words on it, and she was able to tell me the words which I could not understand.

and all the nations shall flow to it,
and many peoples shall come, and say:
"Come, let us go up to the mountain of the Lord,
to the house of the God of Jacob,
that he may teach us his ways
and that we may walk in his paths."
For out of Zion shall go forth the law,
and the word of the Lord from Jerusalem.
He shall judge between the nations,
and shall decide disputes for many peoples;
and they shall beat their swords into plowshares,
and their spears into pruning hooks;
nation shall not lift up sword against nation,
neither shall they learn war anymore"
Isaiah 2:2-4 ESV.

Jerusalem, on your southern wall,
A watchman has stood and has walked,
A released a song of lament from Ireland
Drifting over the ancient stones,
Down into the streets below,
Entering windows and doors,
Houses and schools,
A song of weeping
A lament of familial discord.

You shall go out and hear of the need of the children,
You need a father's heart,
A heart to weep and cry for the youth.
But first, you need to dance,
And then you shall see the eight harps release a sound.
Now the time has come to go out beyond the city,
A time is coming to fight giants,
Just like when David stopped to pick up five stones,

So, shall you also pick stones from the brook[329].
There you shall see the camps where the armies stood,
And gain an understanding for the days ahead.
And you shall turn from defence to attack.
Lord, bring me to the trees where I can find healing,
For my clan and my nation,
Set us on the right path,
And reestablish a call to prayer.
Lord, You know the desert that I have entered
The dryness of my failures and shortcomings,
Help my people, Lord,
But as for me, I am not worthy,
But I will do whatever You ask of me.
The flaming sword has cut through to the truth.
I thought that the well was within sight[330],
But I have now seen how deep it is,
And know, O God I know, I must go deeper still.
Lord, I repent, release me to go deeper,
Release me to have joy.
Lord, You are a strong tower,
Where I can take shelter from the heat,
You release a fresh wind over us,
That brings relief.
And I saw a vision of a golden boat headed to the nations,
On a river of golden glory.
You bring me again to the high places[331],
To hear a song that You play over me,
You put my hands to work.

"In that day, 'A pleasant vineyard, sing of it!
I, the Lord, am its keeper;

---

329 Visited the riverbed during Sukkot 2019.

330 Revelation at the well of Beersheba.

331 Tower at Beersheba.

every moment I water it.
Lest anyone punish it,
I keep it night and day'"
Isaiah 27:2-3 ESV.

"You destroy those who speak lies;
the Lord abhors the bloodthirsty and deceitful man"
Psalms 5:6 ESV.

"O God, why do you cast us off forever?
Why does your anger smoke against the sheep of your pasture?
Remember your congregation, which you have purchased of old,
which you have redeemed to be the tribe of your heritage!
Remember Mount Zion, where you have dwelt.
Direct your steps to the perpetual ruins;
the enemy has destroyed everything in the sanctuary!
Your foes have roared in the midst of your meeting place;
they set up their own signs for signs.
They Were like those who swing axes
in a forest of trees.
And all its carved wood
they broke down with hatchets and hammers.
They set your sanctuary on fire;
they profaned the dwelling place of your name,
bringing it down to the ground.
They said to themselves, "We will utterly subdue them";
they burned all the meeting places of God in the land.
We do not see our signs;
there is no longer any prophet,
and there is none among us who knows how long.
How long, O God, is the foe to scoff?
Is the enemy to revile your name forever?
Why do you hold back your hand, your right hand?
Take it from the fold of your garment and destroy them!
Yet God my King is from of old,

working salvation in the midst of the earth.
You divided the sea by your might;
you broke the heads of the sea monsters on the waters.
You crushed the heads of Leviathan;
you gave him as food for the creatures of the wilderness.
You split open springs and brooks;
you dried up ever-flowing streams.
Yours is the day, yours also the night;
you have established the heavenly lights and the sun.
You have fixed all the boundaries of the earth;
you have made summer and winter.
Remember this, O Lord, how the enemy scoffs,
and a foolish people reviles your name.
Do not deliver the soul of your dove to the wild beasts;
do not forget the life of your poor forever.
Have regard for the covenant,
for the dark places of the land
are full of the habitations of violence.
Let not the downtrodden turn back in shame;
let the poor and needy praise your name.
Arise, O God, defend your cause;
remember how the foolish scoff at you all the day!
Do not forget the clamour of your foes,
the uproar of those who rise against you,
which goes up continually!" Psalm 74:1-23 ESV.

Lord, You bring me to the ancient place of negotiation,
To the site of the brotherly covenant of Tyre and Israel,
The area of the 'burning of the waters'[332].
You have shown me this place,
The place of the cave, and the wave,

332 Book of Joshua mentions 'Misraphet Mayim'.

And the hidden diamonds to be unveiled[333].
And yet, You bring into focus thoughts of the innocent[334],
You care for those who are in the crib,
You watch over the blood of the innocent,
And stand against the deception[335] in my nation.
Shall we see a knight on the bridge
Shouting that no one shall pass[336]?

Psalm 104 ESV[337]

"O Lord My God, You Are Very Great
Bless the Lord, O my soul!
O Lord my God, you are very great!
You are clothed with splendour and majesty,
covering yourself with light as with a garment,
stretching out the heavens like a tent.
He lays the beams of his chambers on the waters;
he makes the clouds his chariot;
he rides on the wings of the wind;
he makes his messengers winds[338]*,*
his ministers a flaming fire.
He set the earth on its foundations,
so that it should never be moved.
You covered it with the deep as with a garment;
the waters stood above the mountains.
At your rebuke they fled;

---

333 Seen in a vision on June 28th 2019.

334 18 is the Hebrew word for 'life', or 'new life'.

335 Double 18 18 means deception or shedding of innocent life.

336 A vision by an intercessor in Galilee during Sukkot 2019.

337 Verses from Psalm 104 were displayed at Rosh Hanikra, also the number 104 stood out because of the 104 fires in Lebanon which had sparked off at same time as the thunder storm in Israel. See news article from 15th October 2019: Fires spread through parts of Lebanon, Syria https://www.arabnews.com/node/1569101/middle-east

338 The wind at BeerSheba.

at the sound of your thunder[339] they took to flight.
The mountains rose, the valleys sank down
to the place that you appointed for them.
You set a boundary that they may not pass[340],
so that they might not again cover the earth.
You make springs gush forth in the valleys;
they flow between the hills;
they give drink to every beast of the field;
the wild donkeys quench their thirst.
Beside them the birds of the heavens dwell;
they sing among the branches.
From your lofty abode you water the mountains;
the earth is satisfied with the fruit of your work.
You cause the grass to grow for the livestock
and plants for man to cultivate,
that he may bring forth food from the earth
and wine[341] to gladden the heart of man,
oil[342] to make his face shine
and bread to strengthen man's heart.
The trees[343] of the Lord are watered abundantly,
the cedars of Lebanon that he planted.
In them the birds build their nests;
the stork has her home in the fir trees.
The high mountains are for the wild goats;

---

339 Thunderstorm in Israel, see article in Jerusalem Post: https://www.jpost.com/Israel-News/Sukkah-sleepers-soaked-by-thunderstorms-throughout-Israel-604672

340 Like the vision of a knight, the leaflet read: "In the summer of 1944, Jewish refugees from the concentration camps were brought to Israel by means of the train that passed through the Rosh Hanikra tunnels. They were exchanged for German citizens of Templar extraction who were living in Eretz Israel whose sons served in the Nazi army. To prevent the passage of Lebanese weapons and soldiers into the territory of the country slated to arise, fighters of the Carmelite division of the Haganah blew up the bridge suspended above the big grotto-opening on a stormy night in March 1948."

341 The wine mentioned at the worship event in Jerusalem.

342 The oil we had come across many times including watching oil being harvested at Beersheba.

343 I had come to Israel, to go to the trees.

the rocks are a refuge for the rock badgers[344].
He made the moon to mark the seasons;
the sun knows its time for setting.
You make darkness, and it is night,
when all the beasts of the forest creep about.
The young lions roar[345] for their prey,
seeking their food from God.
When the sun rises, they steal away
and lie down in their dens.
Man goes out to his work
and to his labour until the evening.
O Lord, how manifold are your works!
In wisdom have you made them all;
the earth is full of your creatures.
Here is the sea, great and wide[346],
which teems with creatures innumerable[347],
living things both small and great.
There go the ships[348],
and Leviathan, which you formed to play in it.
These all look to you,
to give them their food in due season.
When you give it to them, they gather it up;
when you open your hand, they are filled with good things.
When you hide your face, they are dismayed;
when you take away their breath, they die
and return to their dust.
When you send forth your Spirit, they are created,
and you renew the face of the ground.
May the glory of the Lord endure forever;

---

344 *Rosh Hanikra is where the rock badgers live.*

345 *The roar of the lion prevalent in recent prophecy and songs.*

346 *We read this Psalm while looking out on the Mediterranean Sea at Rosh Hanikra.*

347 *The fish which swam towards the sound.*

348 *Out to sea we saw war ships doing manoeuvres.*

may the Lord rejoice in his works,
who looks on the earth and it trembles,
who touches the mountains and they smoke[349]!
I will sing to the Lord as long as I live;
I will sing praise to my God while I have being.
May my meditation be pleasing to him,
for I rejoice in the Lord.
Let sinners be consumed from the earth,
and let the wicked be no more!
Bless the Lord, O my soul!
Praise the Lord!"

You take me into the depths of the mountain,
Where You carved out a path,
For the captives to be set free,
Listen, can you hear the sound of freedom?
Then down into the caves, You led me,
And the sound of freedom went out into the water,
And fish swam closer.
The wave Lord, send an enormous wave!
And the sound went forth into the water
To release the wave.
Then I put my hand upon the roof,
And once again I saw the vision of the diamonds,
And suddenly they popped
And turned into gold dust,
A treasure had been released.
Lord, You will act to help the innocent!
Please help the innocent of my land.
You cause a treasure to bubble up,
You send a fresh breeze of relief[350].

---

349 The fires of Lebanon, as above.

350 Ps 31:17-20 ESV "O Lord, let me not be put to shame, for I call upon you; let the wicked be put to shame; let them go silently to Sheol. Let the lying lips be mute, which speak insolently against the righteous in pride and

Four years to await the harvest.
There are four years of sieges when you come into the land[351].
Then I saw the words, "Consider it done[352]".

You drew us to the ancient place,
And in ancient times,
Some of my people came through Europe,
Killing and stealing from their brother,
And came here to the unconquered city[353]
A central port,
A place of rendezvous,
And put it to siege[354].
Lord forgive my people,
The time has come for full alignment,
The crowns You have set before us,
Forgive our treatment of our brother.
Its time to let it all go,
To release the fourteen cities and the wall,
Out of my hand and into yours,
To be carried away by a big wave.
The walls have been strengthened.

Just like Nehemiah,
You have shown me the state of the walls,
But now I need a vision.
Lead me up onto the mountain[355],
Open the doors,

---

contempt. Oh, how abundant is your goodness, which you have stored up for those who fear you and worked for those who take refuge in you, in the sight of the children of mankind! In the cover of your presence you hide them from the plots of men; you store them in your shelter from the strife of tongues.

351 See Isaiah 5 & Matt 21.

352 Strangely written on the car that had parked in front of us.

353 Akko is on the list of unconquered cities in the time of Joshua, see Judges 1:31.

354 Four years of siege which ended in 1104 (First Crusade).

355 Mt Carmel.

And draw me to the place
Where I can seek Your Face.
Give me a vision Lord,
Of how the innocent can be saved.

"Blessed are the peacemakers,
for they shall be called sons of God" Matthew 5:9 ESV.

Once again You have brought me to the high places[356],
Early in the morning will I seek thee,
Grant me the wisdom of Your marvellous ways,
Keep me, Lord, on Thy path for my life.
Look I see the sunrise come.
The night has been cold,
The dew rests on Your banquet table.
People stand and await the coming glory.
In the dark, they know not which
Way to stare.
But now dark separates from light,
And the sun begins to pierce,
The sound of anticipation as the
Birds sing out among the trees.
Your ways are glorious.
Your name is majestic.
You are beautiful.
Your wonders cease not.
I love You Lord
More than anything!
Lord, You have measured my heart
And found it wanting.
I have not been in deep
Communion with you, but I fell asleep.
And so, I am deeply sorry,

---

356 On the rooftop of a Jerusalem hotel 19th Oct 2019.

I was caught up in the strife
Of this magnifying life,
Learning on my eyes' sight
And not Your Might.
Set me on a path
Where the snare is not
And where sin is forgotten.
Lead me along
And give me a new song.
You've been here all along.
Cover me with tender mercies
Shower me with an embrace,
As I turn this day and seek Your Face.

"All the paths of the Lord are steadfast love and faithfulness,
for those who keep his covenant and his testimonies"
Psalm 25:10 ESV.

The doors are open
And the brothers come in.
Once apart
But now together
As Christ's Church[357].
I sit in the porch and see
A messianic congregation.
The doors are open!
The doors are open
And the assembly begins
From Israel, they come
From Jerusalem, they come
From the nations, they come.
I have seen it
And am overcome.

---

357 Twin doors, Christ Church near Jaffa Gate, 19th October 2019.

Lord, this began when You showed me the closed doors,
        And now, You have shown me that they are open[358].

"It is the Lord who goes before you.
He will be with you;
        he will not leave you or forsake you.
                Do not fear or be dismayed"
                        Deuteronomy 31:8 ESV.
"I am the vine; you are the branches.
Whoever abides in me and I in him,
        he it is that bears much fruit,
                for apart from me you can do nothing" John 15:5 ESV.

I see the valley[359]
        And the blood there-in
                Convicted and guilty
                        Innocent blood did run.
The judgement came for all, not the one
        By the hand of Assyria.
Broken, rejected for their rejection
        Spread amongst the camp
                Like an infection.
Carried away to captivity.
It all happened so suddenly.
The travail of the innocent and guilty
        Was heard in the valley.
The oppressor shall return
        As the victim
                And shall be brought low
                        Before God Almighty.
Lord, I place a petition before
        Your court,

---

358 Comparing the doors in Basel Switzerland to the doors in Israel.

359 Valley of Hinnom, Israel.

Do not allow my people into
The valley of Hinnom.
To see their sin put
As a yoke on their neck.
Instead, Lord show Your Mercy –
I believe my people will turn.
Will You destroy a nation if
ten righteous men are in it?
If wickedness prevails,
Then my Lord,
Let Your Right Hand
Tear the mountains
And shred the high places!
But while there are those
Who seek Your Face,
Hold back Thy judgement.
I ask for something special
A miracle,
I know, only you, only you,
Lord can do it.
Do You hear my petition, Lord?
Will You come and save?
Use me, Lord – I am willing!
Rise up the generations,
Shoulder to shoulder,
A family
Focused on You and
Your love,
That Your glory will be evident
Once again in the nation
Of Ireland.
Then I saw a strategy that God was releasing
To save the innocent of Ireland.